Editor

Lorin Klistoff, M.A.

Managing Editor

Karen Goldfluss, M.S. Ed.

Illustrator

Renée Christine Yates

Cover Artist

Barb Lorseyedi

Art Director

CJae Forshay

Art Manager

Kevin Barnes

Imaging

Rosa C. See

Publisher

Mary D. Smith, M.S. Ed.

READING, LANG...

ACTIVITIES
FALL

Grades K–2

How much does the backpack cost?

3¢

All About Me!

Author

Mary Rosenberg

Teacher Created Resources

Teacher Created Resources, Inc.

6421 Industry Way

Westminster, CA 92683

www.teachercreated.com

ISBN-1-4206-3888-2

©2005 Teacher Created Resources, Inc.

Made in U.S.A.

Table of Contents

Introduction

How to Use This Book

The activities in *Reading, Language & Math Activities: Fall* are designed to grab the students' interest and engage the students in wanting to learn more. The activities are hands-on, fun-filled, and allow students of different academic levels to be successful. All of the activities have been kid-tested and teacher-approved.

The activities can be used in a variety of ways in the primary classroom. The games and activities can be done with the whole class, in small groups, with a partner, independently, or placed at a center. Many of the games and activities can be sent home with the student to play with his or her family. This reinforces the home-school connection and shows the student's family what is being taught in the classroom.

The activities can be played in small groups with students of differing abilities and are non-competitive in nature. The activities were designed this way so that the students would enjoy practicing important math or language arts skills without worrying about which person is the smartest one.

The activities are also great to use with English language learners. The pictures help the student to understand what he or she is supposed to do and supports the student in learning the names of items and comprehending the material.

This book has been divided into five self-contained units. Each unit has its own table of contents, thematic activities and games, and answer key.

Writing Domains

All students need to write across the domains, in a variety of genres, and to fit specific purposes. This can be accomplished through daily writing practice and guided writing instruction.

- **Practical/Informative:** This domain can be considered "just the facts." This type of writing tells how to do something—such as writing a recipe, the steps for making a bed, or how to fill out a party invitation. (*Example:* Write the steps for giving a dog a bath.)

- **Analytical/Expository:** This domain can be considered the "convince me" form of writing. This type of writing answers a "why" or "how" question about a specific topic. The writer expresses an idea, thought, or opinion and provides supporting evidence. (*Example:* Tell why Crunchy Flakes are better than Crispy Flakes.)

- **Imaginative/Narrative:** This domain of writing is frequently used with primary age students. The writer might retell a favorite story with a new ending, tell about a familiar event, or make up a story about a favorite character. (*Example:* Pretend an eraser could talk. What would the eraser say?)

- **Sensory/Descriptive:** This domain has the student describe a certain event, object, person, or memory using words that allow the reader to create visual pictures in his or her mind. (*Example:* Describe how a hot fudge sundae tastes.)

Writing Journals

Just about anything can be used as a writing journal. Some suggestions are as follows: spiral notebooks, composition books, theme or seasonal-shaped writing paper, notepads, blank paper, lined paper, or sticky notes. You can even die-cut sheets of paper and staple the papers into individual booklets. Generic writing paper for each writing level is provided on pages 6–8.

Introduction

Sentence Frames

At the beginning of the school year, write a sentence frame on a piece of paper and photocopy it for the students. To make it easier for the students to see and follow your modeling, write the sentence frame on a sentence strip or make it into an overhead transparency. As a class or as a small group, complete the sentence frame. Some sample sentence frames are as follows:

- We go to _____ School.
- I live in a _____.
- My favorite color is _____.
- My name is _____.

Encourage the more capable writers to go beyond the sentence frame and write an additional sentence or two on the topic.

As the students become more confident and proficient writers, sentence frames will not be needed. However, the students need to see the classroom teacher model and use good writing every day!

K-W-L Charts

A K-W-L chart is a great way to introduce a new writing topic to the students. By using a K-W-L chart, the students are learning to organize information, develop questions about the topic that can serve as a guide to learning, and use the information (both previously known and newly learned) in their writing. A K-W-L chart is provided on page 9. Make an overhead transparency of the K-W-L chart and fill it in as a class. If desired, provided each student with a photocopy of the filled-in (or partially completed) K-W-L chart to keep in his or her writing folder.

Word Banks

Word banks can be a rich resource for students to use when writing on a specific topic or theme. Word banks can be written on one of the theme-related writing pages. They can be photocopied for the students to use, put on a chalkboard, an overhead projector, or on a seasonal-shaped piece of butcher paper. The words in the word bank are intended to push the student to write beyond "I like . . . ." If the student is using at least one of the words in the word bank in each sentence, the student's writing will be more interesting to read. It will challenge the student to incorporate new words and phrases into his or her writing.

Two sample word banks are shown below. The first Word Bank contains just words. The second Word Bank has used clip art to illustrate each word. (Stickers, stamps, or drawings can also be used in place of clip art.) The illustrations make it easier for younger students to read and use the words in their writing.

Word Bank					
fire	lantern	tent	flashlight	logs	trees

Word Bank					
fire	lantern	tent	flashlight	logs	trees

Introduction

Informal Writing Evaluation

Writing can be scored in many different ways. One way to quickly check the student's mechanics of writing is to use a checklist. The checklist can include capital letters, punctuation (periods, question marks, exclamation points), spelling (usually high frequency words and CVC words), and using sentences that answer several of the 5 W + H questions (*who*, *what*, *where*, *when*, *why*, and *how* questions). Use the blank check-off list on page 10 to help you.

Provide feedback to the student regarding his or her writing. Show the student an area of weakness that needs to be addressed (such as beginning each new sentence with a capital letter) and an area that has shown improvement (such as using sentences that answer some of the 5 W + H questions).

Formal Writing Evaluation

A formal rubric can also be used to monitor the student's writing progress over the course of the school year. Below is a sample of a formal writing rubric.

4 Points: Exceptional Writer

- Begins each sentence with a capital letter
- Ends each sentence with a period, question mark, or exclamation point
- Capitalizes proper nouns
- Uses a variety of sentence structures to make the writing interesting to read
- Spells high-frequency words with CVC words correctly
- Takes risks in his or her writing
- Writes several sentences on the topic

3 Points: Competent Writer

- Regularly begins a sentence with a capital letter and ends each sentence with a period, question mark, or exclamation point
- Capitalizes proper nouns
- Spells many high-frequency words and CVC words correctly
- Writes more than one sentence on the topic

2 Points: Developing Writer

- Starting to begin each sentence with a capital letter
- Starting to use a period, question mark, or exclamation point at the end of the sentence
- Spells words phonetically—writing the beginning, middle, and/or ending sounds heard in the word
- Attempts to write at least one sentence on the topic
- "Reads" his or her writing to an adult

1 Point: Beginning Writer

- Writes using a string of random letters
- May or may not "read" his or her writing to an adult

_____

(Title)

_____

- -

_____

_____

- -

_____

_____

- -

_____

- -

_____

_____

- -

_____

7

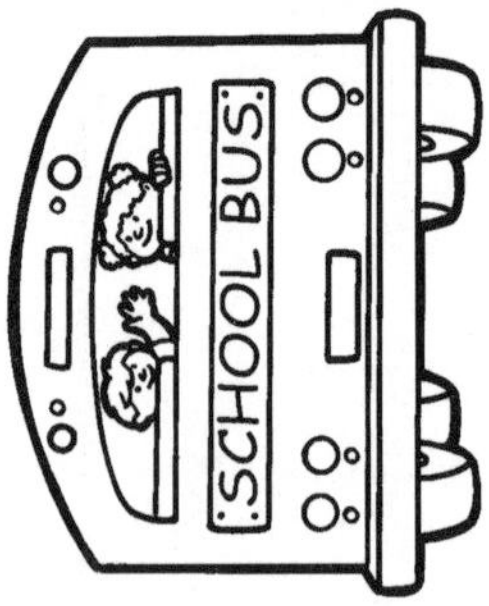
SCHOOL BUS

K-W-L Chart

Subject: _____

What We Know	What We Would Like to Learn	What We Did Learn

Check-Off List

1.										
2.										
3.										
4.										
5.										
6.										
7.										
8.										
9.										
10.										
11.										
12.										
13.										
14.										
15.										
16.										
17.										
18.										
19.										
20.										
21.										
22.										
23.										
24.										

About Me

Table of Contents

About Me

Introduction

About Me contains activities that are great for "breaking the ice" and for getting to know more about a student and his or her family.

Reading and Language Activities

- **Check-Off List (page 10):** Use the blank check-off list to keep track of each language and reading activity as it is completed by the student.

- **About Me Cover (page 14):** Simply photocopy the pages the students are to do and use this page as the cover for this short unit. Or photocopy the appropriate level of writing paper on pages 6–8 for each student and staple them to the cover to make a writing packet.

- **About Me Writing Prompts (page 15):** Writing prompts for each one of the four domains are provided. The writing prompts are a fun way to get to know more about the students in the class.

- **True Statements About Me (page 16):** Students cut out the true statements that apply to their situations. The true statements are then glued into the box, and then students write more true statements about themselves.

- **About Me (page 17):** Students cut out the words about family and glue them in alphabetical order. Students then answer questions regarding the words that are in alphabetical order.

- **Letter Matches (pages 18–20):** These cut-and-paste activities reinforce identifying and matching uppercase and lowercase letters. Students cut out the "puzzle pieces" at the bottom of the page and glue them in place under the matching uppercase letter. If done correctly, the letters will spell a word and a picture will be revealed.

- **All in the Family (page 21):** Students search for family words in a word search.

- **My Life (pages 22–25):** This is an activity that can be worked on by the student throughout the year. Photocopy the pages into individual packets for each student. As the school year progresses, the students can complete the packet. At the end of the year, display the completed autobiographies at Open House. (This is also a fantastic way to showcase the progress in writing that the students made over the course of the school year.)

About Me

Math Activities

- **Family Pets (page 26):** This is a logic activity. Read the clues and place Xs or Os in the appropriate boxes. Once an O has been placed in a box, Xs must be placed in any remaining boxes in that same row and column. (*Note:* An O means that the person can do or have a particular task or item. Nobody else can have it.)

- **Mystery Relative (page 27):** This activity can be done more than just one time! Make an overhead transparency of this page. Explain to the students that one of the relatives just robbed a bank (or walked the dog, or ate the last cookie, etc.). Have the students ask you questions in order to find out who is the mystery relative. (The students need to ask questions that can be answered with "yes" or "no.") As each question is answered, cross off any pictures that fit the criteria.

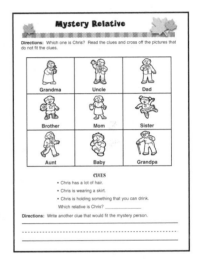

- **Brothers, Sisters, and Pets (page 28):** This activity has each student make a graph and complete sentences about his or her own family. This activity can be extended to make a graph about the whole class. The class graph could show the following: number of students who have a brother(s), number of students who have a sister(s), number of students who have a pet(s).

- **Growing Up! (page 29):** This is a sequencing activity. The student can select to sequence either the boy pictures or the girl pictures (or both!). Once the student has selected a set of pictures, he or she cuts them out and glues them in the correct order. (If doing both sets of pictures, the second set of pictures can be glued to the back of the page.)

- **Who Matches Me? (page 30):** Students will use the skill of comparing while doing this great ice-breaker activity. Each student tries to find a classmate who fits one of the criteria listed on the page. The classmate then writes his or her name on the line on the other student's page.

- **My Body (page 31):** Students will enjoy using a measuring tape to measure the parts of their bodies.

- **My Bedroom (page 32):** This activity has the student make a map of his or her bedroom (or even his or her ideal bedroom). Photocopy this page onto cardstock or construction paper. Have the student cut out the items found in his or her bedroom. The items can be glued onto a piece of cardstock or construction paper. To make it more realistic, use the inside of a shoebox! (The sides of the shoebox can represent the walls of the bedroom.) The students can use location words (left, right, next to, beside, in between, on top of, under, etc.) to describe the location of items in the bedroom.

About Me

About Me Writing Prompts

Domain	Writing Prompt	Word Bank
Practical/Informative	My Family	aunt, brother, dad, mom, sister, uncle
Practical/Informative	Where I Live	apartment, condominium, house, mobile home, share room
Analytical/Expository	Things I Like	With the students, brainstorm a list of items and/or things that they like.
Analytical/Expository	Things I Don't Like	With the students, brainstorm a list of items and/or things that they do not like.
Imaginative/Narrative	This is What My House Would Say About Me	fun, messy, neat, noisy, plays, quiet, rooms, runs around, snores, watches TV
Imaginative/Narrative	Favorite Stuffed Animal or Pet (A Day Spent at School with You)	With the students, brainstorm a list of activities or feelings the stuffed animal or pet might have if brought to school for the day.
Sensory/Descriptive	My Bedroom	big, clean, closet, messy, share room, small, toy box, window
Sensory/Descriptive	About Me	eyes, favorite color, hair, long, short, years old

True Statements About Me

Directions: Cut out the small boxes at the bottom of the page. Glue the true statements about yourself in the box below.

Directions: Write another true statement about yourself.

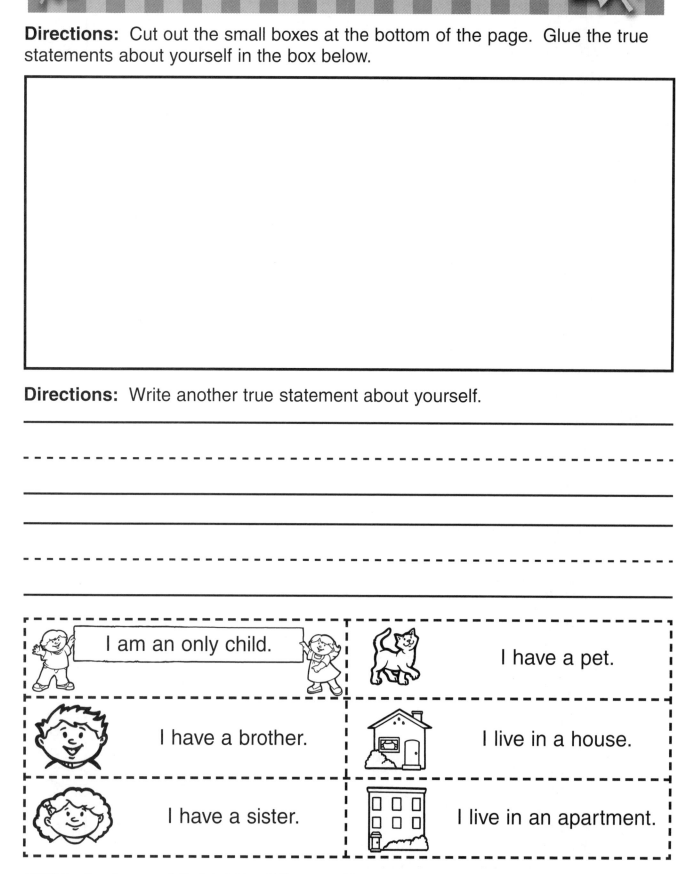

I am an only child.

I have a pet.

I have a brother.

I live in a house.

I have a sister.

I live in an apartment.

About Me

Directions: Cut out the words at the bottom of the page. Put the words in alphabetical order and then answer each question.

1.

2.

3.

4.

5.

6. Which word is <u>first</u>?

_____

7. Which word comes <u>after</u> *Dad*?

_____

8. Which word comes <u>before</u> *sister*?

_____

9. Which word is <u>last</u>?

_____

10. Which word is <u>second</u>?

_____

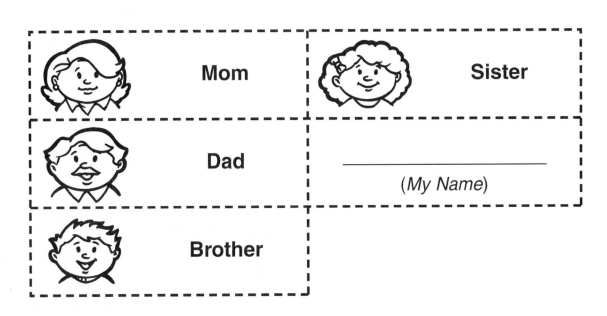

Mom

Sister

Dad

_____
(*My Name*)

Brother

Letter Match

Directions: Cut out the boxes at the bottom of the page. Glue each lowercase letter box to the matching uppercase letter box to find a picture.

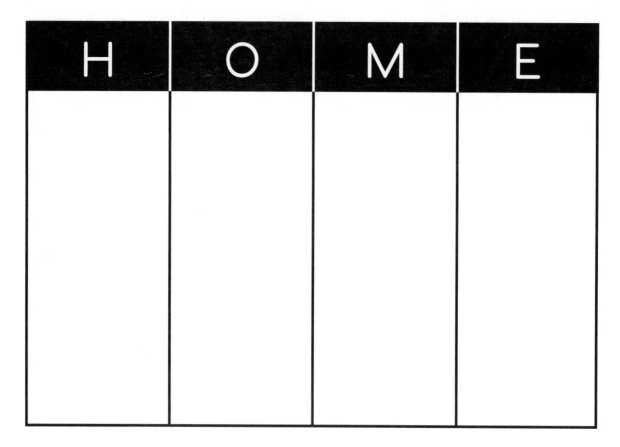

H	O	M	E

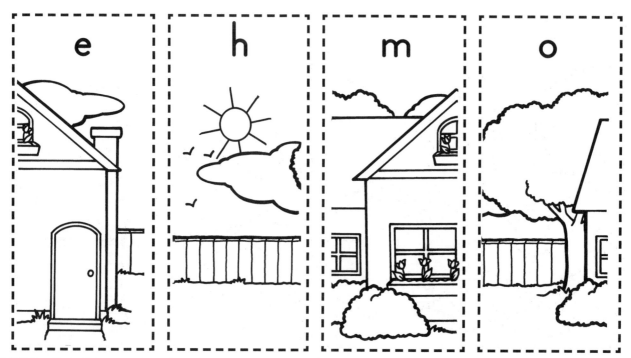

e   h   m   o

Letter Match

Directions: Cut out the boxes at the bottom of the page. Glue each lowercase letter box to the matching uppercase letter box to find a picture.

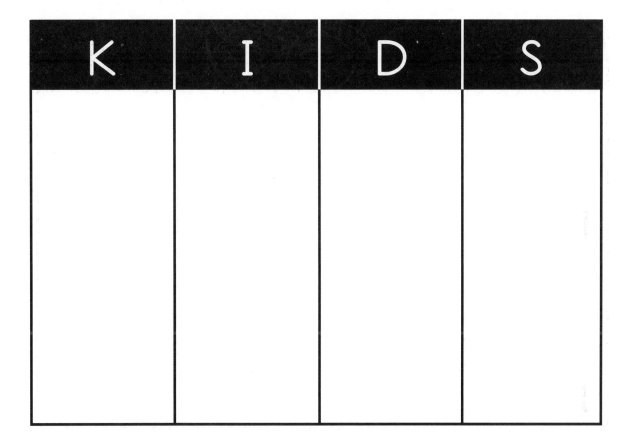

Letter Match

Directions: Cut out the boxes at the bottom of the page. Glue each lowercase letter box to the matching uppercase letter box to find a picture.

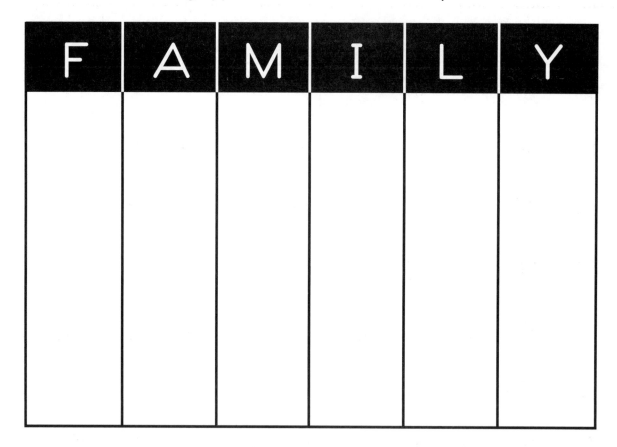

F	A	M	I	L	Y

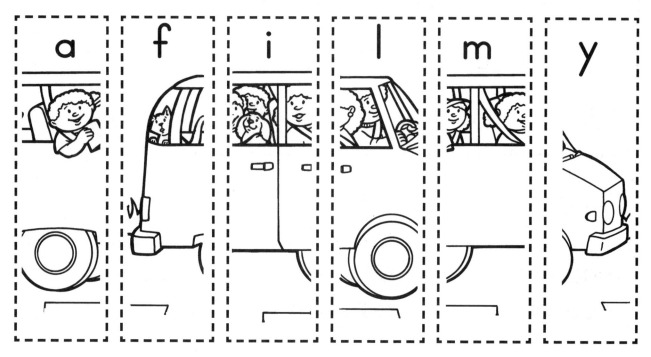

All in the Family

Directions: Find and color each word.

```
G  R  A  N  D  M  A  A  B  C
F  A  T  H  E  R  Q  Z  R  D
U  N  C  L  E  Y  A  U  N  T
M  O  T  H  E  R  J  K  A  E
N  N  I  E  C  E  T  X  S  F
M  B  I  H  S  I  S  T  E  R
L  C  U  G  R  A  N  D  P  A
N  E  P  H  E  W  W  F  G  G
B  A  B  Y  C  O  U  S  I  N
J  I  B  R  O  T  H  E  R  H
```

AUNT	FATHER	NEPHEW
BABY	GRANDMA	NIECE
BROTHER	GRANDPA	SISTER
COUSIN	MOTHER	UNCLE

My Life

by _____

When I Was Little

Right Now

In the Future

Family Pets

Directions: Read each clue. If the answer is "yes," make an **O** in the box. If the answer is "no," make an **X** in the box.

	Cat	Dog	Rabbit	Fish
Mom				
Dad				
Brother				
Sister				

CLUES

- Mom does not feed any animals with fur.
- Sister feeds an animal that hops.
- Dad feeds the cat.

Which family member feeds each pet?

 1. Mom feeds the _____.

 3. Brother feeds the _____.

 2. Dad feeds the _____.

 4. Sister feeds the _____.

Mystery Relative

Directions: Which one is Chris? Read the clues and cross off the pictures that do not fit the clues.

Grandma	Uncle	Dad
Brother	Mom	Sister
Aunt	Baby	Grandpa

CLUES

- Chris has a lot of hair.

- Chris is wearing a skirt.

- Chris is holding something that you can drink.

Which relative is Chris? _____

Directions: Write another clue that would fit the mystery person.

_____

- -

_____

Brothers, Sisters, and Pets

Directions: Make a graph and complete the sentences about your family.

	1	2	3	4	5	6	7
Brothers							
Sisters							
Pets							

I have _____ brothers.

I have _____ sisters.

I have _____ pets.

Growing Up!

Directions

1. Select a set of pictures at the bottom of the page.

2. Cut the pictures out.

3. Put the pictures in order from youngest to oldest.

4. Glue the pictures into the boxes below.

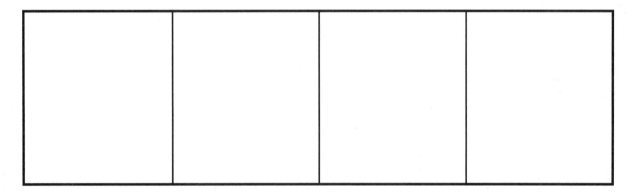

youngest ⟶ oldest

Set 1

Set 2

Who Matches Me?

Directions: Find a classmate who . . .

1. is the same height   _____

2. has the same color of eyes   _____

3. has the same color of hair   _____

4. is wearing the same color of shirt   _____

5. was born in the same month   _____

My Body

Directions: Use a measuring tape to measure each body part.

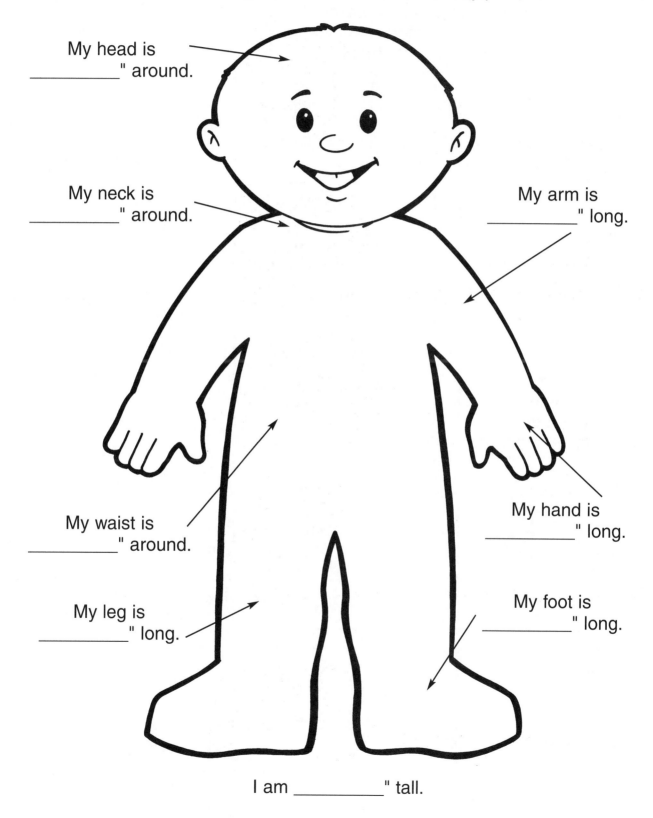

My head is _____" around.

My neck is _____" around.

My waist is _____" around.

My leg is _____" long.

My arm is _____" long.

My hand is _____" long.

My foot is _____" long.

I am _____" tall.

My Bedroom

Directions: Make a map of your bedroom or your ideal bedroom. Cut out the items found in the bedroom. Glue the pieces onto paper. To make it more realistic, use the inside of a shoebox! (The sides of the shoebox can represent the walls of the bedroom.) Create more pieces to add to your bedroom.

Fold on line
and glue here.

Fold on line
and glue here.

Fold on line
and glue here.

Fold on line
and glue here.

Fold on line
and glue here.

Fold on line
and glue here.

Fold on line
and glue here.

Fold on line
and glue here.

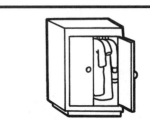

Fold on line
and glue here.

Fold on line
and glue here.

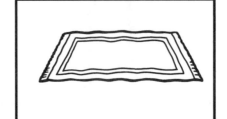

Fold on line
and glue here.

Fold on line
and glue here.

Answer Key

Page 16

Answers will vary.

Page 17

Answers will vary depending on name of student.

Page 18

Page 19

Page 20

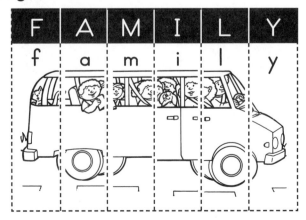

Page 21

G	R	A	N	D	M	A	A	B	C
F	A	T	H	E	R	Q	Z	R	D
U	N	C	L	E	Y	A	U	N	T
M	O	T	H	E	R	J	K	A	E
N	N	I	E	C	E	T	X	S	F
M	B	I	H	S	I	S	T	E	R
L	C	U	G	R	A	N	D	P	A
N	E	P	H	E	W	W	F	G	G
B	A	B	Y	C	O	U	S	I	N
J	I	B	R	O	T	H	E	R	H

Page 26

Page 27

Mom

Page 29

Set 1

Set 2

About School

Table of Contents

About School

Introduction

Each of the About School activities contains a school theme.

Reading and Language Activities

- **About School Cover (page 37):** Simply photocopy the cover and the appropriate writing paper on pages 6–8 for each student and staple them together for a writing packet. Or, photocopy all the activities in this school unit and attach the cover to them.

- **Check-Off List (page 10):** This can be used to keep track of each activity as it is completed by the student.

- **About School Writing Prompts (pages 38 and 39):** Writing prompts for each one of the four domains are provided. The writing prompts are a fun way to find out more about the students and how they feel about school.

- **At School (page 40)** and **School Rules (page 41):** These are cut-and-paste activities. Students sort the words or sentences into the appropriate categories and then write a true statement about one of the categories.

- **Letter Matches (pages 42–44):** These cut-and-paste activities reinforce identifying and matching uppercase and lowercase letters. The students cut out the "puzzle pieces" at the bottom of the page and glue them in place under the matching uppercase letter. If done correctly, the letters will spell a word and a picture will be revealed.

- **A Day at School (page 45):** Students will certainly learn classroom vocabulary by doing this activity. Students place words about school items into a crossword puzzle.

- **School House Bingo (pages 46–48):** Bingo is always a hit with the students. This bingo is great for English Language Learners (ELL), because it reinforces the names of commonly used school tools. As an extension activity, make two photocopies of the calling cards (page 48) and use the cards to play Concentration.

- **Kid Concentration (page 49):** Kid Concentration is a fun game for a student to play with a partner when he or she has a few extra minutes before going to recess or lunch, when he or she finishes his or her work early, or before going home at the end of the day. For each group of kids, photocopy two sets of the Kid Concentration cards. Each set of cards can be stored in a small, plastic bag.

- **Glue (page 50)** and **Crayons (page 51):** These pages provide basic information about school tools used by everybody—glue and crayons! After reading the information, there are a few questions for students to answer.

About School

Math Activities

- **School Tools Graph (page 52)**, **How We Get to School (page 53)**, and **Boys and Girls in Our Class (page 54):** Read or create a graph using the students' information and then answer questions about the graph.

- **School Supplies (page 55):** Students will identify out how much each school item costs.

- **Pencil Measuring (page 56):** Students use non-standard measurement to measure different items on the page.

- **Are They Symmetrical? (page 57):** Students must figure out whether each line drawn through a face is symmetrical or not.

- **Numbers on the Bus (page 58):** This activity provides the students with practice in reading number words to ten. Cut out the buses at the bottom of the page. (Each bus should be cut in half on the broken line.) Then glue each number word on top of the matching number. When completed, the number words should be in order going from 1 to 10. Below the school buses, write the number word next to each number.

- **Time for Recess! (pages 59 and 60):** This activity provides the students with practice in reading numbers and number words to five. Make a photocopy of the game board and its playing pieces for each group (2–4) of students. Each set of game pieces can be stored in a large mailing envelope or large baggie.

- **4 Bells in a Row (pages 61–64):** This activity provides the students with practice in counting items to 10. Make a photocopy of the game board and its playing pieces for each group (2–4) of students. When cutting out the pieces, make sure to cut around the "kid dominoes" instead of cutting each domino in half. (Each domino consists of two small squares.) Each set of game pieces can be stored in a large mailing envelope or large baggie. There is a blank playing board provided. Extension Ideas: On the blank playing board write the number words for the numbers 6 to 10 and then play the game as usual!

- **School Tools Dominoes (page 65):** Photocopy one set of dominoes for each small group (2–4) of students. Cut the dominoes apart and place in a stack face down on the table. Each player takes five dominoes. The player with a double gets to go first. The double domino is laid down on the table. The next player then has to match one of the ends of his/her dominoes to the end of the double. If the player is unable to make a match, he or she must take a domino from those still laying face down on the table. The first player to use all of his or her dominoes wins the game.

- **School Puzzle (page 66):** Provide the students with a photocopy of the puzzle and a clean sheet of paper. Have the students cut the puzzle pieces apart and put them together on a clean sheet of paper. Once the puzzle has been completed, the students can glue the puzzle pieces to the sheet of paper.

About School

Town Elementary

SCHOOL BUS

STOP

About School Writing Prompts

Domain	Writing Prompt	Word Bank
Practical/Informative	This year I would like to learn . . .	grade, handwriting, homework, money, reading, spelling, time
Practical/Informative	Last year I learned . . .	carpet time, math, reading, science, stories, teacher
Practical/Informative	How to Make a Friend	fun, hello, nice, share, shake hands, play, recess
Practical/Informative	Make a list of crayon colors.	black, blue, brown, gray, green, orange, pink, purple, red, white, yellow
Analytical/Expository	Which is better—hot lunch or cold lunch?	cafeteria, favorite food, line, lunch pail, milk, money, sack lunch, tray
Analytical/Expository	Recess Fun	bars, basketball, jump, jump rope, play, run, skip, soccer ball, swings, tether ball
Analytical/Expository	Write a good school or classroom rule.	raising hands, learning, principal, running, sharing, students, talking, teacher, walking
Analytical/Expository	Is homework a good idea?	day care, extra practice, helps, learning, parents, play, sports, time, tired

About School Writing Prompts

Domain	Writing Prompt	Word Bank
Imaginative/Narrative	My Favorite Color of Crayon	beautiful, brightest, darkest, flowers, fun, grass, happy, prettiest, sky, warm
Imaginative/Narrative	What is your best memory about school?	arts and crafts, field trip, painting, parents, playing, sharing, snacks
Imaginative/Narrative	Pretend you are a pencil. What is your day like?	breaking, fingers, grabbing, poking, rubbing, sharpening, squeezing, writing
Imaginative/Narrative	Write about your first day in a new grade.	classroom, excited, nervous, new friends, scared, teacher, want to learn
Sensory/Descriptive	Develop a new color of crayon.	amazing, color, fabulous, interesting, invent, kitchen, lab, sparkling
Sensory/Descriptive	Describe the perfect classroom.	books, chairs, crayons, cubbies, desks, faucets, furniture, pencils, rugs
Sensory/Descriptive	What does a brand new book smell like? Feel like?	clean, crackles, crisp, pages, sharp, smells, smooth, stiff
Sensory/Descriptive	What does it feel like to swing on a swing?	bird, butterflies, clouds, exciting, flying, free, stomach

At School

Directions: Cut out the words at the bottom of the page. Then glue them below under the correct title.

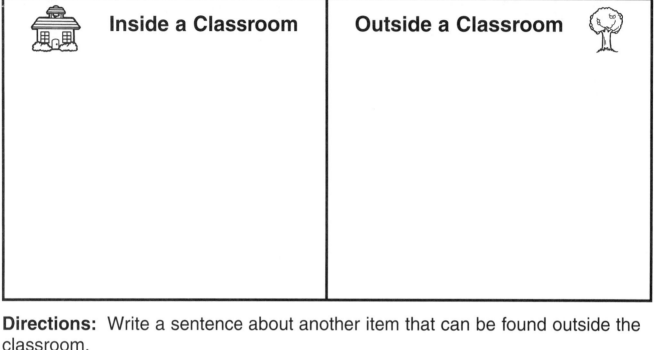Inside a Classroom	Outside a Classroom

Directions: Write a sentence about another item that can be found outside the classroom.

_____

- -

_____

_____

- -

basketball hoop	computer
scissors	bus
swing	globe

School Rules

Directions: Cut out the words at the bottom of the page. Then glue them below under the correct title.

Good School Rules	Bad School Rules

Directions: Write another good school rule.

_____

- -

_____

- -

Play nicely with the other students.	Hit or trip classmates.
Call people names.	Share materials with classmates.
Say kind words to others.	Run in the hallways.

Letter Match

Directions: Cut out the boxes at the bottom of the page. Glue the lowercase letter box to the uppercase letter box to find a picture.

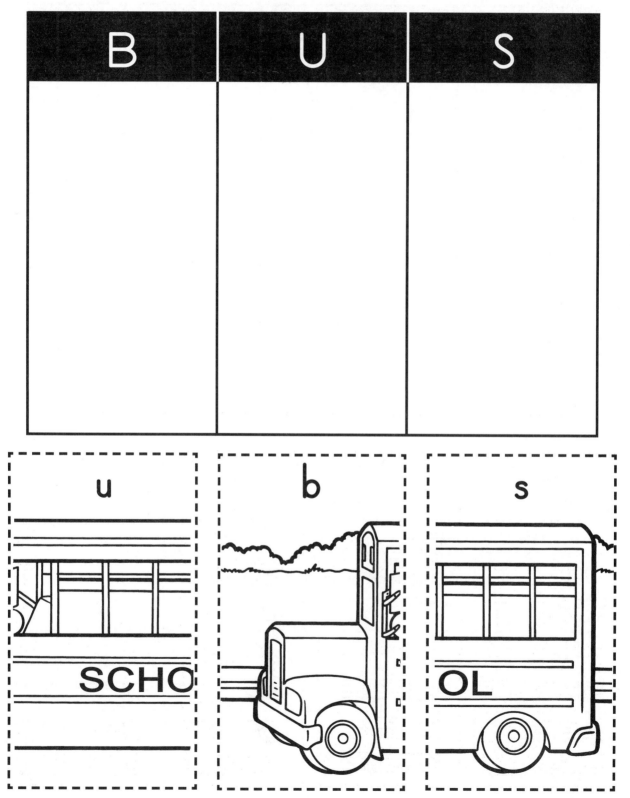

B   U   S

u   b   s

SCHO   OL

Letter Match

Directions: Cut out the boxes at the bottom of the page. Glue the lowercase letter box to the uppercase letter box to find a picture.

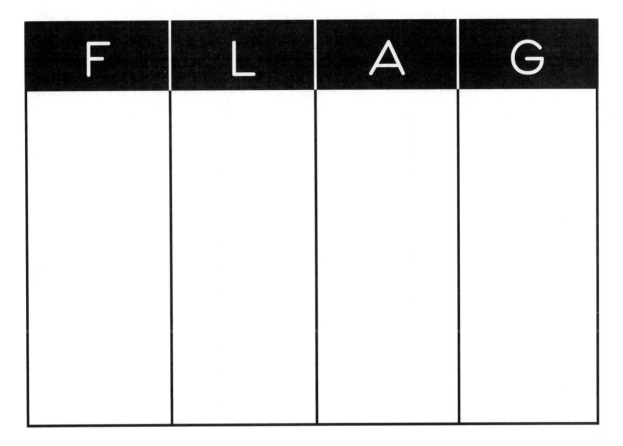

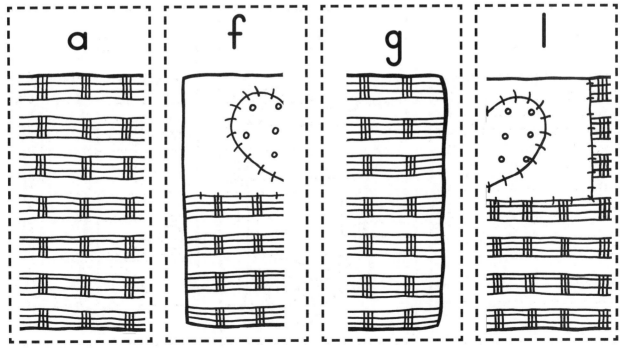

Letter Match

Directions: Cut out the boxes at the bottom of the page. Glue the lowercase letter box to the uppercase letter box to find a picture.

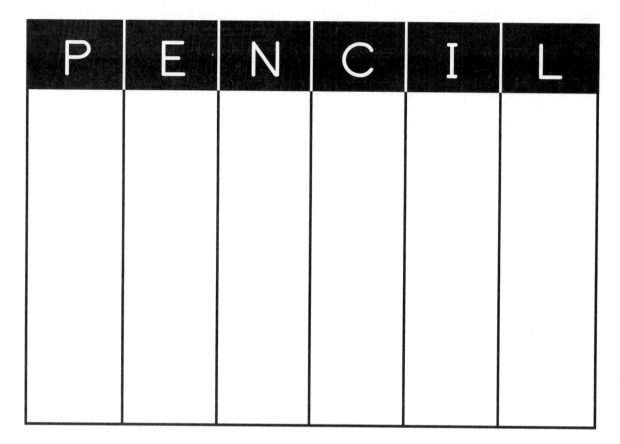

P	E	N	C	I	L

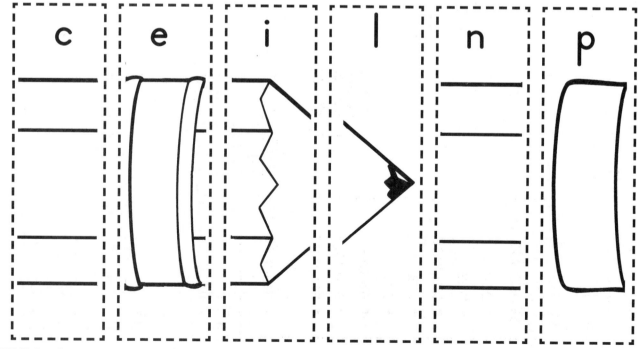

| c | e | i | l | n | p |

A Day at School

Directions: Write the name of each object in the boxes. (One letter in each box.)

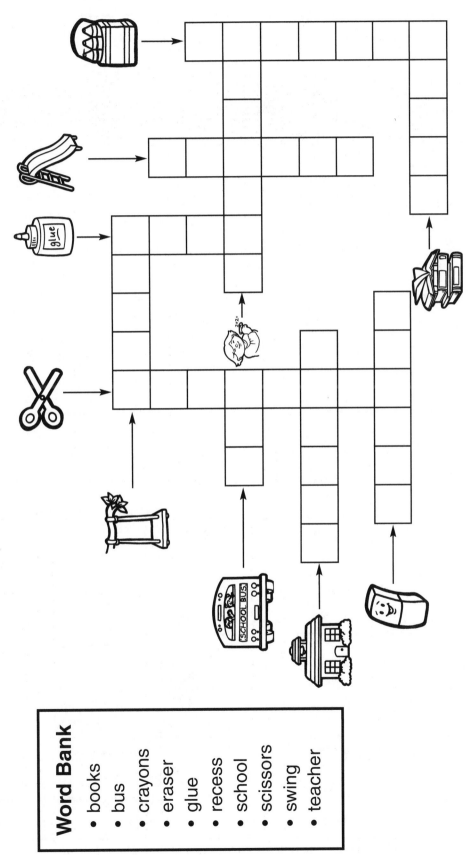

Word Bank
- books
- bus
- crayons
- eraser
- glue
- recess
- school
- scissors
- swing
- teacher

Bingo Boards

Card 1

School House Bingo

bus	backpack	books
crayons	Free Space	bell
computer	pencil	lunch

Card 2

School House Bingo

read	pencil	ruler
books	Free Space	bus
crayons	computer	backpack

Card 3

School House Bingo

paste	read	bell
books	Free Space	scissors
backpack	pencil	lunch

Card 4

School House Bingo

computer	bus	lunch
scissors	Free Space	bell
ruler	read	paste

Bingo Boards

School House Bingo

lunch	scissors	paste
read	Free Space	books
ruler	pencil	computer

School House Bingo

backpack	crayons	computer
bell	Free Space	pencil
paste	books	scissors

School House Bingo

crayons	ruler	backpack
scissors	Free Space	paste
lunch	bus	bell

School House Bingo

bell	scissors	read
bus	Free Space	crayons
computer	pencil	ruler

Bingo Calling Cards

bus	crayons	pencil
paste	scissors	books
bell	ruler	backpack
lunch	read	computer

Kid Concentration

Dan

Jan

Al

Lynn

Bob

Sue

Tim

Bea

Glue

Directions: Read the information in the box and answer the questions below.

In 1947 the first white glue was made. The glue was called "Elmer's Glue-All."

Glue is made of "sticky" polymers. The glue becomes hard because the air dries all of the water out of it.

If the tip of the glue bottle becomes clogged, let it soak in warm, soapy water. The water will loosen the glue and then the tip is as good as new!

1. In what year was the first white glue made?

1497 ○   1947 ○   1749 ○

2. What was its original name?

Elmer's Glue ○   Elmer's Glue-It ○   Elmer's Glue-All ○

3. Why does the glue become hard?

The glue is sticky ○   The water is dried out of it. ○   The air is dry. ○

4. What should you do if the glue tip becomes clogged?

Let it soak in water. ○   Pick at it. ○   Cut it with scissors. ○

Crayons

Directions: Read the information in the box and answer the questions below.

> Binney & Smith made the first box of crayons in 1903. The box cost 5¢ and had eight crayons.
>
> During the Great Depression, Binney & Smith hired farm families to hand-label each crayon. Each farm did one crayon color. Pretty soon each farm became known by the color of crayons they wrapped.
>
> In 1996, Binney & Smith sold their 100 billionth crayon!

1. Who made the first box of crayons?

    Crayola Crayons   Binney & Smith   Farm Families
        ◯   ◯   ◯

2. How many crayons were in the first box of crayons?

       six   four   eight
       ◯   ◯   ◯

3. What did the farm families become known by?

   their crayon color   their farm animals   their crops
        ◯   ◯   ◯

4. In what year was the 100 billionth crayon sold?

      1996   2006   1896
       ◯   ◯   ◯

School Tools Graph

Directions: Use the graph to answer the questions.

	✏️			
	pencil			
	pencil	scissors		
	pencil	scissors		
eraser	pencil	scissors		crayons
eraser	pencil	scissors		crayons
eraser	pencil	scissors	glue	crayons

1. Write the number for each item.

 _____ _____  _____ _____ _____

2. Are there more pencils or erasers? Circle your answer.

3. Are there fewer crayons or scissors? Circle your answer.

4. Which two have the same number of items? Circle your answer.

How We Get to School

Directions: Ask the students in your classroom how they get to school. Record their answers on the graph, and then answer the questions.

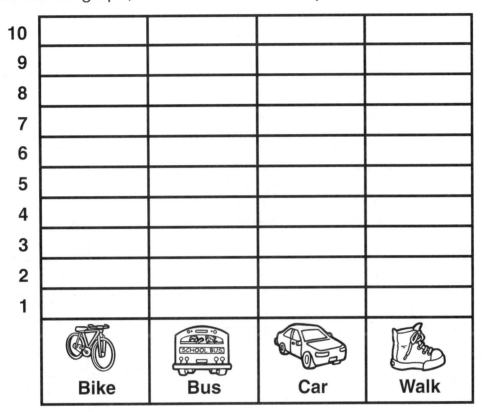

	Bike	Bus	Car	Walk
10				
9				
8				
7				
6				
5				
4				
3				
2				
1				

1. Write the number.

 _____ _____ _____ _____

2. Do more kids or ?

3. Do fewer kids or ?

4. How many kids and ? _____

5. How many kids and ? _____

6. What is your favorite way to get to school? _____

Boys and Girls in Our Class

Directions: Find out how many boys and girls are in your class. Record the answers on the graph, and then answer the questions.

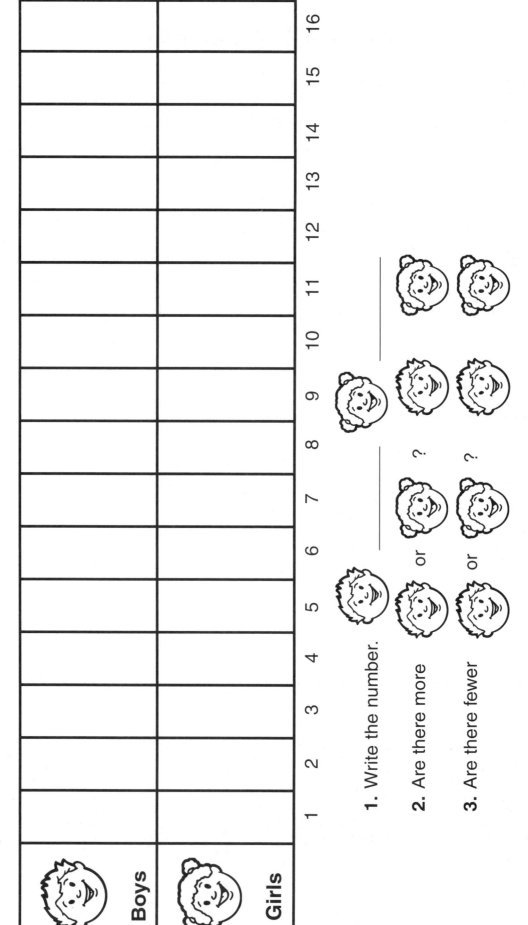

	1	2	3	4	5	6	7	8	9	10	11	12	13	14	15	16
Boys																
Girls																

1. Write the number. _____

2. Are there more _____ or _____ ?

3. Are there fewer _____ or _____ ?

4. How many students are in the class? _____

School Supplies

Directions: Write the cost of each item on the line.

1.

_____ ¢

2.

_____ ¢

3.

_____ ¢

4.

_____ ¢

5.

_____ ¢

6.

_____ ¢

Pencil Measuring

Directions: Cut out the pencil ruler. Use the ruler to measure the length of each item.

1.

The box of crayons is _____ pencils long.

2.

The pennant is _____ pencils long.

3.

The troop of girls is _____ pencils long.

4.

The team of boys is _____ pencils long.

Pencil Ruler

Are They Symmetrical?

Directions: Circle "yes" if the picture is symmetrical. Circle "no" if the picture is not symmetrical.

1. yes no	**2.** yes no	**3.** yes no
4. yes no	**5.** yes no	**6.** yes no
7. yes no	**8.** yes no	**9.** yes no
10. yes no	**11.** yes no	**12.** yes no

Numbers on the Bus

Directions: Cut out each bus half at the bottom of the page. Then match each number word to its number.

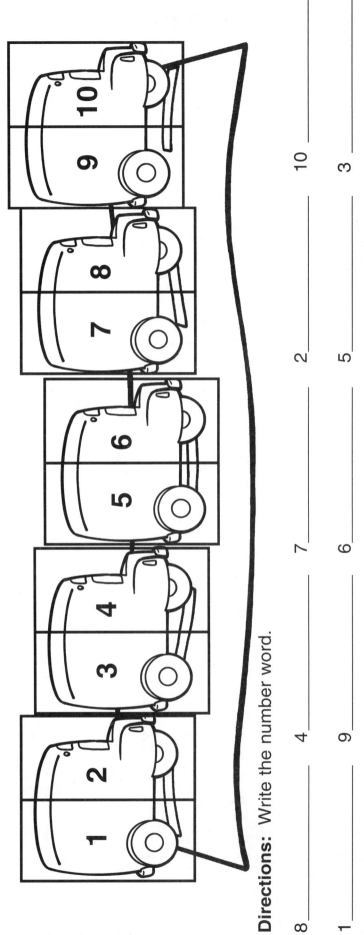

Directions: Write the number word.

8 _____

1 _____

4 _____

9 _____

7 _____

6 _____

2 _____

5 _____

10 _____

3 _____

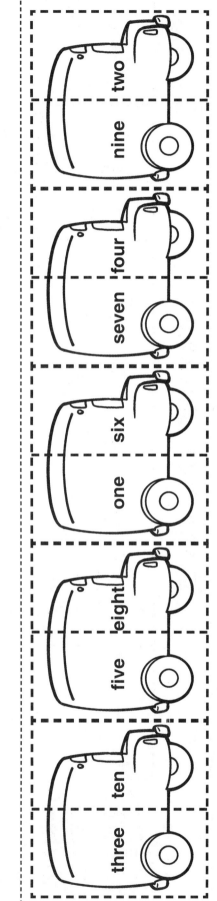

Time for Recess!

2	1	3	4	5

4	0			

5	3	2		

START

Number of Players: 2–4 students

Materials: 1 playing board and game pieces for each group of students

Directions: Taking turns, each student turns over a number card and moves his or her number to the nearest matching number. If you land on the space at the top of the slide, slide down to the space below it. If you land on the same space as another player, the other player gets bumped back to start. The first player to reach the playground wins the game!

2	0	4	1	3

5	2	0	4	3

FINISH

Time for Recess! Playing Pieces

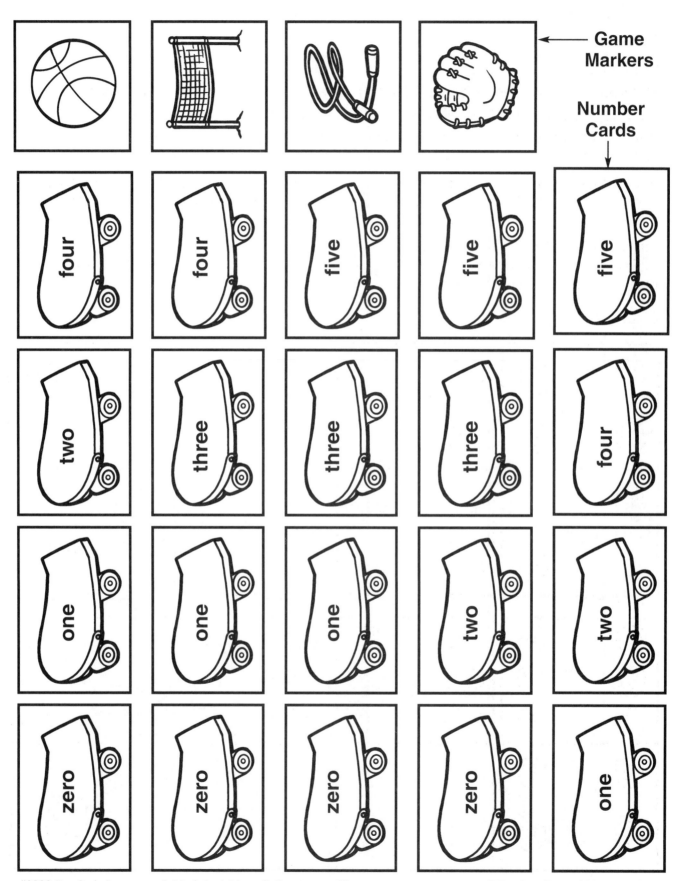

Game Markers

Number Cards

4 Bells in a Row

Directions

Number of Players: 2 students

Materials: 1 playing board for each student and 1 set of the kid dominoes for both players.

To Play: Taking turns, each student turns over a domino, counts the number of kids, and places a bell on the matching number on his or her playing board. The first student to have four bells in a row (vertically, horizontally, or diagonally) wins the game.

Variation #1: Give each student a blank school house. Have the student fill in the boxes using the numbers 6, 7, 8, 9, 10. (Each number can be repeated several times.) Play the game using the same directions outlined above.

Variation #2: Give each student a blank school house. Have the student write a different addition or subtraction problem that equals 6, 7, 8, 9, or 10 in each space. Play the game using the same directions outlined above.

Game Pieces

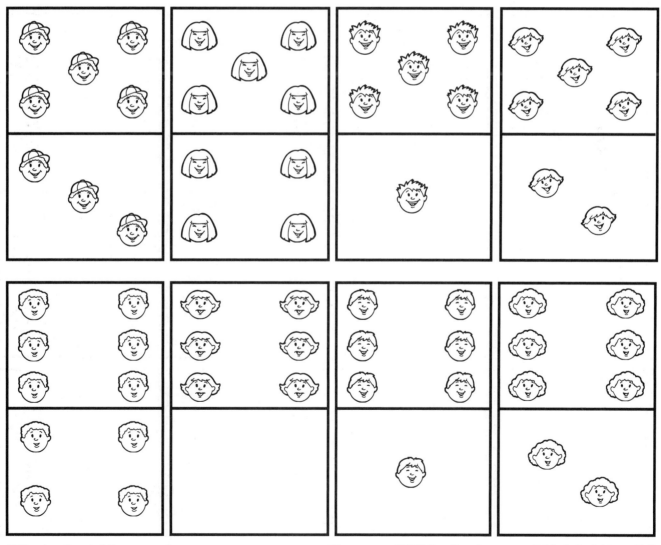

4 Bells in a Row

Game Pieces *(cont.)*

4 Bells in a Row

School Tools Dominoes

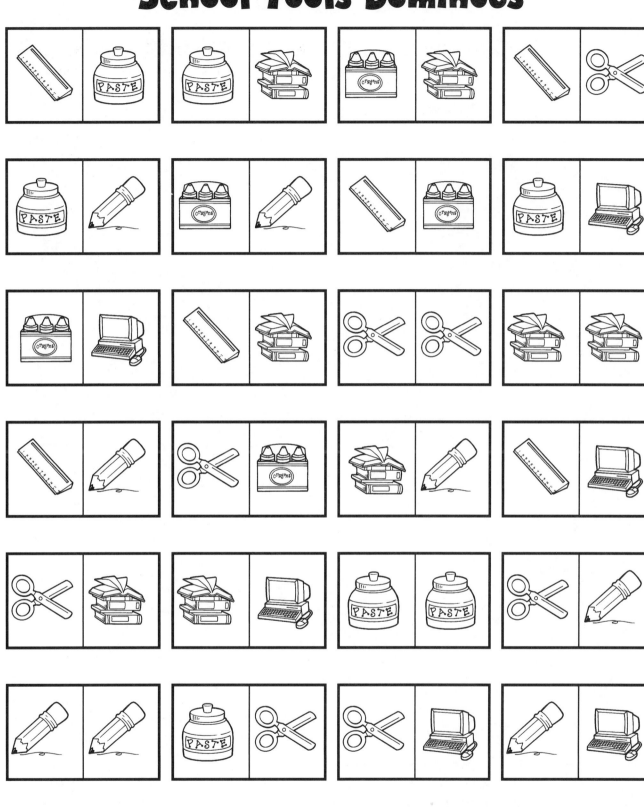

Page 40

Inside a Classroom: scissors, computer, globe

Outside a Classroom: basketball hoop, swing, bus

Answers will vary for the sentence.

Page 41

Good School Rules: Play nicely with the other students. Say kind words to others. Share materials with classmates.

Bad School Rules: Call people names. Hit or trip classmates. Run in the hallways.

Answers will vary for another good school rule.

Page 42

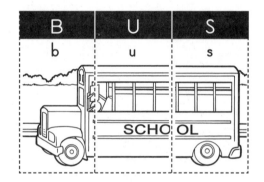

Page 43

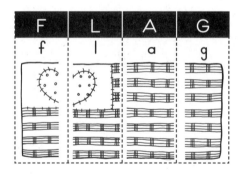

Page 44

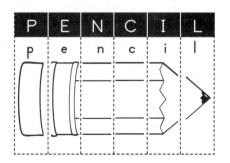

Page 45

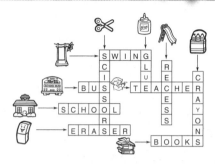

Page 50

1. 1947   2. Elmer's Glue-All
3. The water is dried out of it.
4. Let is soak in water.

Page 51

1. Binney & Smith   3. their crayon color
2. eight   4. 1996

Page 52

1. 3, 3, 5, 1, 6   2. Circle pencil.
3. Circle crayons.
4. Circle crayons and eraser.

Page 55

1. 3¢	3. 5¢	5. 5¢
2. 4¢	4. 1¢	6. 2¢

Page 56

1. 1   2. 2   3. 5   4. 4

Page 57

1. yes	4. no	7. no	10. yes
2. no	5. no	8. yes	11. no
3. yes	6. no	9. no	12. no

Page 58

Make sure number words on the cars are correctly matched to the number on the cars.

8 = eight, 4 = four, 7 = seven, 2 = two, 10 = ten

1 = one, 9 = nine, 6 = six, 5 = five, 3 = three

Page 66

About Apples

Table of Contents

About Apples

Introduction

About Apples contains activities and games that are all about apples. The activities introduce basic information about apples as well as provide a variety of games and activities that introduce and practice basic skills covered in the primary grades.

Reading and Language Arts Activities

- **About Apples Cover (page 72):** Simply photocopy the pages the students are to do and use this page as the cover for this unit. Or, photocopy sets of the writing paper for each student and staple to make a writing packet. The About Apples Cover can be used as the cover for the writing packet.

- **Check-Off List (page 10):** This can be used to keep track of each activity as it is completed by the student.

- **About Apples Writing Prompts (pages 73 and 74):** Writing prompts for each one of the four domains are provided. The writing prompts are a fun way to explore the world of apples!

- **Apples (pages 75)** and **Candied Apples (page 76):** Each activity has the students sort statements into two different categories.

- **Order of Apples (page 77):** Students are sure to enjoy placing apple vocabulary in the correct alphabetical order.

- **Johnny Appleseed (page 78):** Students will learn about the life of Johnny Appleseed doing this activity. Pages can be cut apart and then stapled to make a mini-booklet.

- **Letter Matches (pages 79–82):** These cut-and-paste activities reinforce indentifying and matching uppercase and lowercase letters. The students cut out the "puzzle pieces" at the bottom of the page and glue them in place under the matching uppercase letter. If done correctly, the letters will spell a word and a picture will be revealed.

- **Making Statements and Questions (page 83):** This activity contains rebus-like pictures and high-frequency words. The students cut apart the words and pictures and arrange and rearrange the words and pictures to make different questions and statements. When doing this activity with the whole class, an overhead transparency of the page can be made or use a photocopy machine to enlarge the words and pictures so that they can be easily seen by all of the students. Some sample sentences that can be made are as follows:

  - I ate the apples.
  - I see the apples.
  - The apple is on the tree.
  - Who ate the apple?

- **How Many Word Can You Make? (page 84):** The students cut apart the letter cards and arrange and rearrange the letters to make different words. When doing this activity with the whole class, make an overhead transparency of the page. Call on individual students to use the overhead to show the class a word he or she has made. This is also a great activity to send home as homework. Sample words that can be made are as follows:
  - 2 letters: as, ad
  - 3 letters: pad, ape, sad, lap, eel, pea
  - 4 letters: peel, seal, seed, sled, sped, slap, deal, peal, peas, sale, pale, leap
  - 5+ letters: apple, please, lease, speed, pedal

About Apples

Reading and Language Activities *(cont.)*

- **The Seeds (pages 85 and 86):** This rebus story activity uses pictures and high frequency words to tell a story. The students can feel successful when they are able to read the story with little or no help from the teacher! The story reads as follows: *The kids dug a hole. The kids put four seeds into the hole. The kids watered the seeds. Every day the kids watered the seeds. One day the seeds began to sprout. The plant grew and grew. Soon it was a tree. The kids picked a basket of apples. The kids ate some of the apples. The kids made a pie and muffins with the rest of the apples.*

- **Apple Word Search (page 87)** and **Apple Picking Time (page 88):** Students will find vocabulary words about apples in a word search or a crossword puzzle.

- **Food Made with Apples (page 89)** and **An Apple Tree (page 90):** In these activities, students will place labels underneath a picture or write the words on a diagram.

- **Apple Bingo (pages 91–93):** This game provides eight different bingo cards and matching calling cards. Apple Bingo reinforces vocabulary and language development skills in a fun-filled, non-threatening manner.

- **The Apple Game (pages 94 and 95):** This game provides practice in naming and identifying the different parts of an apple. Provide a game board (page 94) for each student in a small group (2–4 students). Each group will also need one die (page 95) and some counters. Taking turns, each student rolls the die and covers the matching picture on his or her board. The first student to cover all of the pictures wins the game!

- **Apple History (page 96)** and **Johnny Appleseed (page 97):** These two pages provide the students with basic information on these two topics, as well as a few questions for the students to answer about what they have just read.

Math Activities

- **Favorite Flavor of Apples (page 98)** and **The Real Apple (page 99):** These are logic activities. As each clue is read, the students cross off the pictures that meet (or do not meet) the clue.

- **Plenty of Apples (page 100):** The students read and answer questions about a chart.

- **Apple Sales (page 101):** Students will place pictures on a graph and then answer questions about the graph.

- **How Tall Is Each Tree? (page 102):** Students will use an apple ruler to measure some apple trees.

- **September Calendar (pages 103 and 104):** Students will put together all the different parts of a calendar and then answer some questions about it.

- **Apple Smiles (page 105):** Students will glue all the pieces of the puzzle in the correct place on the graph to form a picture.

- **Apple Sort (pages 106 and 107):** This activity can be done with the whole class. Make an overhead transparency of both pages. Place the large apple transparency (page 107) on the overhead projector. Place several of the pictures inside the apple and the remaining pictures outside the apple. Ask the students, "What is the rule to be in this family?" Call on students to answer. Suggested ways to sort the apples are as follows: apples with stems, apples with leaves, or apples with worms. To extend this activity, provide each student with copies of both pages and have them sort the apples and write the rule.

About Apples

Math Activities (cont.)

- **Apple Patterns (page 108 and 109):** The students will make patterns using apple-related pictures. Photocopy the pattern sleeve onto construction paper, fold, and glue in the back to create the sleeve. For each student, provide three to four 12" lengths of sentence strips. Photocopy a class set of the apple-related pictures. Have the students cut out the pictures and use the pictures to make different patterns on the sentence strips.

- **Apple Puzzle (page 110):** Have the students cut apart the puzzle pieces and arrange the pieces on a clean sheet of paper. This is a great activity to place at a center or for students who finish their work early.

- **Draw the Apple Tree (page 111):** This game requires a six-sided die. Each student will need a copy of this page. In small groups (two to four students), the players take turns rolling the die. If a player rolls a "1," he or she may draw the trunk of the tree. On his or her next turn, this player must roll a "2" before being able to draw the leaves on the tree. The first player to draw a complete tree wins the game. (The numbers must be rolled in sequential order before the student can draw a part of the tree.) The activity has space for four games. Additional games can be played on the back of the page or on a piece of scratch paper.

- **Apple Halves (page 112):** The student cuts out the apples at the bottom of the page and then cuts each apple in half. The student matches each apple's number word to the number on the apple half at the top of the page. This activity reinforces number words and number identification.

- **Counting Apple Seeds (page 113):** Students can count the number of seeds in each apple and then write the number on the lines.

- **Are They Symmetrical? (page 114):** Students will explore the symmetry of apples.

- **Johnny Appleseed Game (pages 115 and 116):** This game reinforces number word and numeral recognition. For each small group (two to four students), photocopy one game board, one set of apples, and one set of game markers.

- **Apple Fractions (pages 117 and 118):** This activity introduces the idea of fractions in a very concrete manner. For each pair of students, provide copies of the apple pictures (cut part) and the spinner. Taking turns, have the students spin the spinner and take the matching apple fraction piece. The student who is able to make the most whole apples wins the game!

- **Four Apples in a Row (pages 119–122):** This game reinforces basic counting skills. A blank playing board is provided for the teacher to use in customizing the game to meet the needs of students who need to work with smaller numbers or for those students who are ready for a more challenging version of the game.

- **Favorite Color of Apples (page 123):** Make a graph showing each student's favorite color of apple. (This activity can be used as a follow-up to the Apple Tasting Chart on page 124.)

- **Apple Tasting Chart (page 124):** This page can be used to record information about different varieties of apples. To do this activity, bring in three different kinds of apples. Show the students each apple and record its variety and size on the chart. (For size, have the students compare each apple to the size of their closed fists. You might decide as a class that a "medium" apple would be the size of a student's fist.) Provide each student with a small sample from one of the apples. Have the students share what the apple tastes like (fresh, sweet, sour, tart, etc.). Record the information on the chart. Repeat this step with the other apple varieties.

About Apples

SEEDS

About Apples Writing Prompts

Domain	Writing Prompt	Word Bank
Practical/Informative	How to Grow an Apple Tree	air, cover, hold, seeds, soil, sunlight, water
Practical/Informative	Johnny Appleseed	apple orchards, John Chapman, Massachusetts, Ohio, planted
Practical/Informative	Nine Ways to Use an Apple	With the students brainstorm a list of different things that can be made (or done) with apples.
Practical/Informative	How to Make Applesauce	apples, bowl, cook, core, peel, pot, seeds, smash, stir
Analytical/Expository	The Best Way to Eat an Apple	bites, honey, peanut butter, plain, slices, whole
Analytical/Expository	My Favorite Apple	apple, green, juicy, red, sour, sweet, yellow
Analytical/Expository	Which apple type is best? Why?	Fuji, Gala, Golden Delicious, Granny Smith, Jonathon, McIntosh, Pippin, Rome
Analytical/Expository	Does an apple a day really keep the doctor away? Why or why not?	clean teeth, freshen breath, fruit, good for you, healthy, snack, vitamins

About Apples Writing Prompts

Domain	Writing Prompt	Word Bank
Imaginative/Narrative	There's a worm!	eat, garbage, refrigerator, scream, yummy
Imaginative/Narrative	You wake up one day and have become an apple. Tell about your day.	bruised, cold, dropped, eaten, lunch, picked, snack, squeezed, worm inside
Imaginative/Narrative	How does an apple keep in shape?	apple, exercise, happy, jumping, rope, shape, smiling
Imaginative/Narrative	What do apples do all day?	become juicy, drop, grow, hang from the branches, sunshine, visit
Sensory/Descriptive	Describe an apple and how it tastes.	bite, delicious, green, juice, red, slices, sour, sweet, whole, yellow
Sensory/Descriptive	The Perfect Apple	crisp, crunchy, delicious, green, juicy, red, sour, sweet, yellow
Sensory/Descriptive	What does an apple tree look like?	apple, blossoms, branches, growing, leafy, trunk
Sensory/Descriptive	A Delicious Treat	baked, cinnamon, cobbler, crumbs, hot, ice cream, juice, pie, sauce

Apples

Directions: Cut out the boxes at the bottom of the page. Then glue them under the correct title, *Facts* or *Opinions*.

Facts	Opinions

Directions: Write another factual statement about apples.

_____

- -

_____
_____

- -

Apples have seeds.	Apples are delicious.
Green apples are my favorite.	Apples grow on trees.
There are many kinds of apples.	I like apples.

Candied Apples

Directions: Cut out the boxes at the bottom of the page. Then glue them under the correct title, *Apples* or *Candied Apples.*

Apples	Candied Apples

Directions: Write a true statement about an apple or a candied apple.

_____

- -

_____

- -

healthy snack	covered in caramel
special treat	comes with a stem
covered with skin	comes on a stick

Order of Apples

Directions: Cut out and glue the picture and word cards in alphabetical order.

1.

2.

3.

4.

5.

half

apples

tree

seeds

core

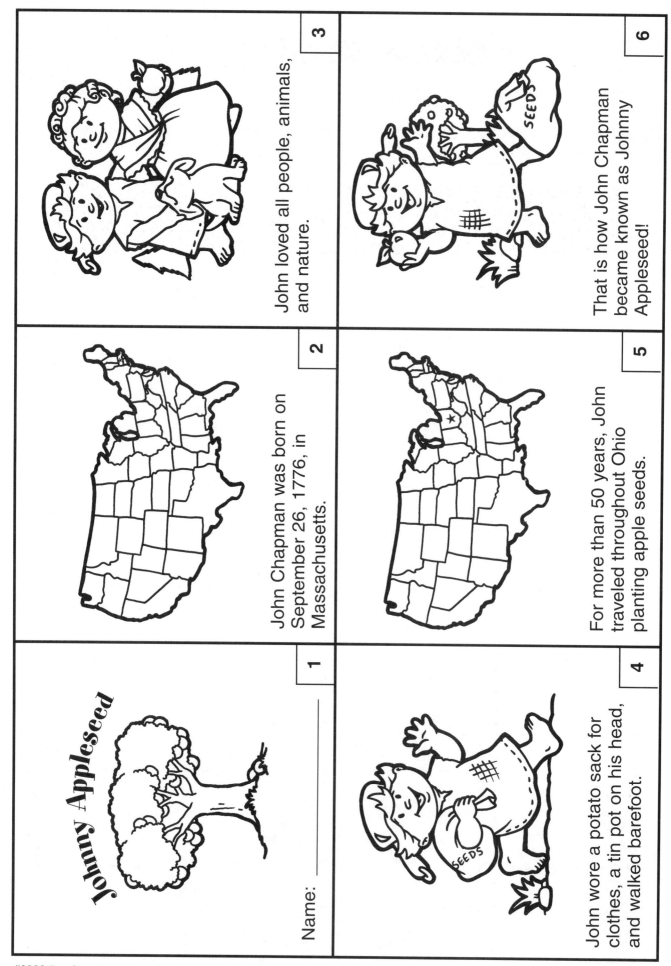

3

John loved all people, animals, and nature.

6

That is how John Chapman became known as Johnny Appleseed!

2

John Chapman was born on September 26, 1776, in Massachusetts.

5

For more than 50 years, John traveled throughout Ohio planting apple seeds.

1

Johnny Appleseed

Name: _____

4

John wore a potato sack for clothes, a tin pot on his head, and walked barefoot.

Letter Match

Directions: Cut out the boxes at the bottom of the page. Glue the lowercase letter box to the uppercase letter box to find a picture.

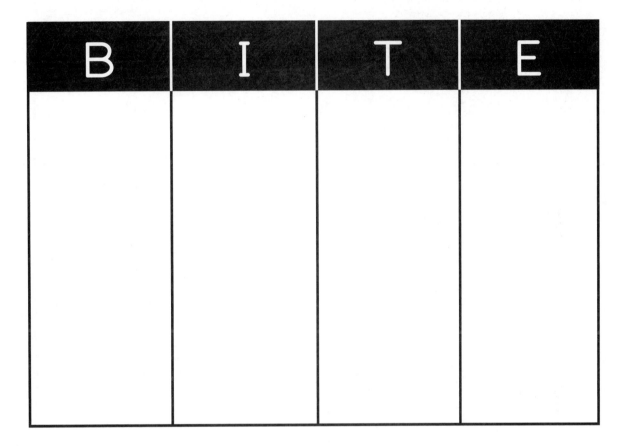

B	I	T	E

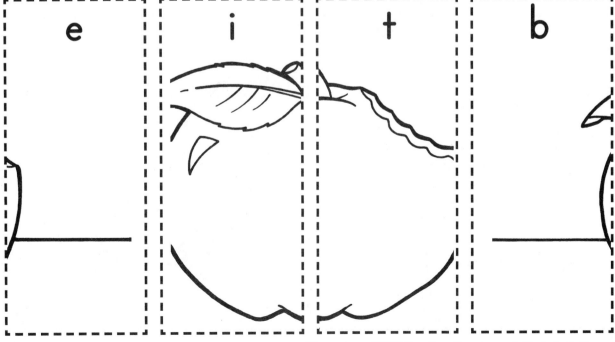

| e | i | t | b |

Letter Match

Directions: Cut out the boxes at the bottom of the page. Glue the lowercase letter box to the uppercase letter box to find a picture.

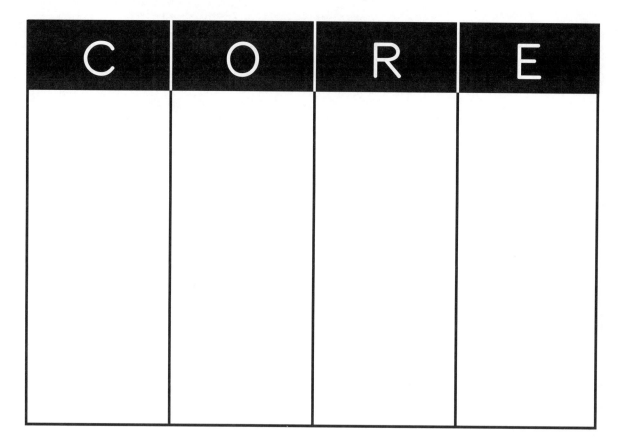

C	O	R	E

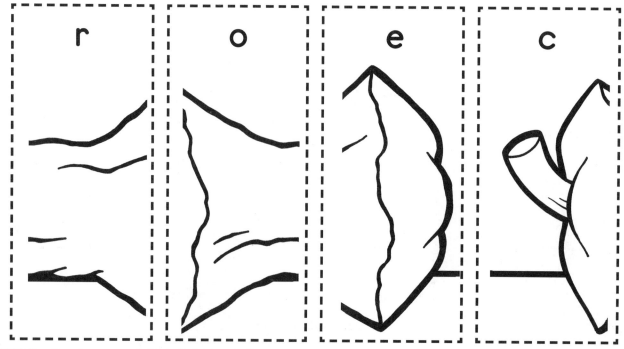

r	o	e	c

Letter Match

Directions: Cut out the boxes at the bottom of the page. Glue the lowercase letter box to the uppercase letter box to find a picture.

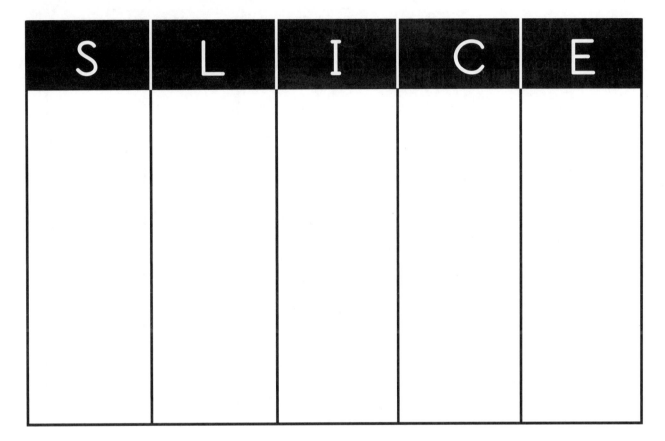

S	L	I	C	E

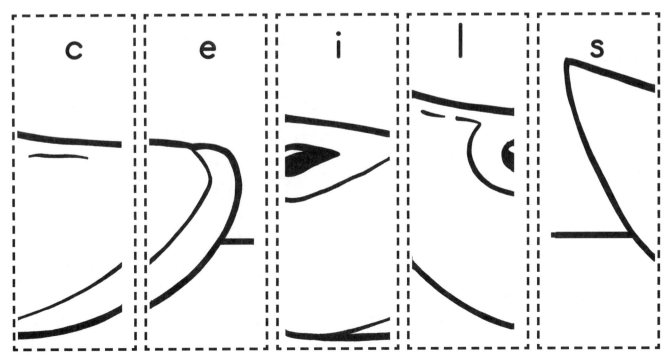

| c | e | i | l | s |

Letter Match

Directions: Cut out the boxes at the bottom of the page. Glue the lowercase letter box to the uppercase letter box to find a picture.

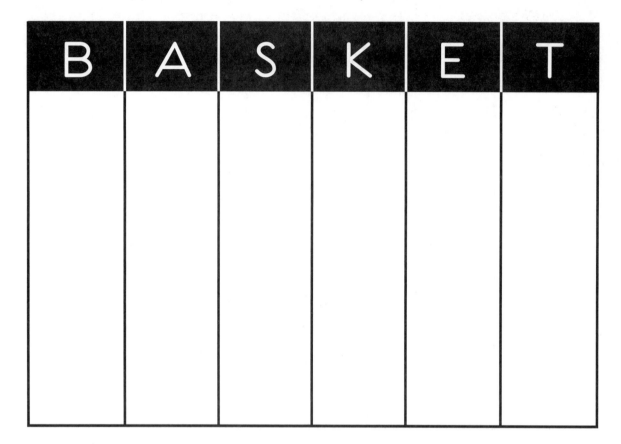

B	A	S	K	E	T

a	b	e	k	s	t

Making Questions and Statements

an	are	.	?
 see	 eight	on	Who
 apple	 basket	Where	is
 apples	 tree	the	has
eat / ate	 fence	I	can

How Many Words Can You Make?

Directions: Cut out the letters at the bottom of the page. Rearrange the letters to make different words. Write each word under the correct heading.

2-Letter Words

3-Letter Words

4-Letter Words

5-or-More Letter Words

a	p	p	l	e	s	e	e	d

The Seeds

The   kids   dug   a   hole.

The   kids   put   four   seeds   into the   hole.

The   kids   watered   the   seeds.

Every   day   the   kids   watered   the   seeds.

One   day   the   seeds   began to   sprout.

The Seeds

The   plant   grew   and   grew.   Soon it was a   tree.

The   kids   picked a   basket   of   apples.

The   kids   ate some of the   apples.

The   kids   made a   pie   and

muffins   with the rest of the   apples.

Apple Word Search

Directions: Find and color each word in the word search.

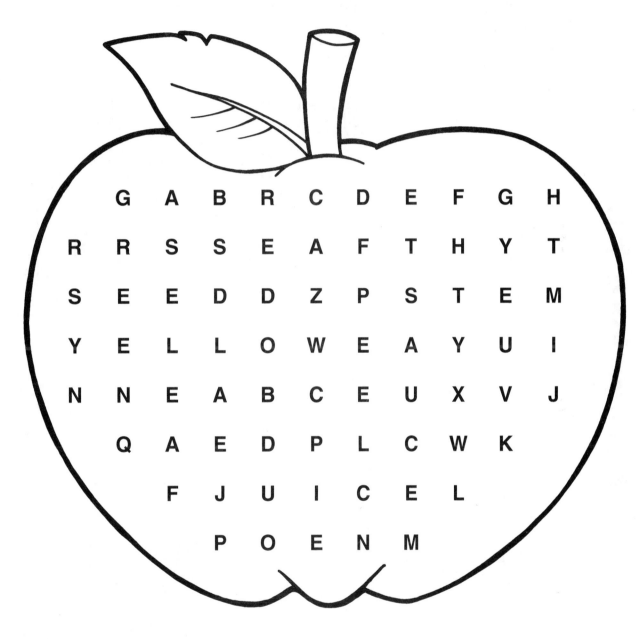

G A B R C D E F G H
R R S S E A F T H Y T
S E E D D Z P S T E M
Y E L L O W E A Y U I
N N E A B C E U X V J
Q A E D P L C W K
F J U I C E L
P O E N M

GREEN   PIE   SEED

JUICE   RED   STEM

LEAF   SAUCE   YELLOW

PEEL

Apple Picking Time

Directions: Complete the crossword puzzle.

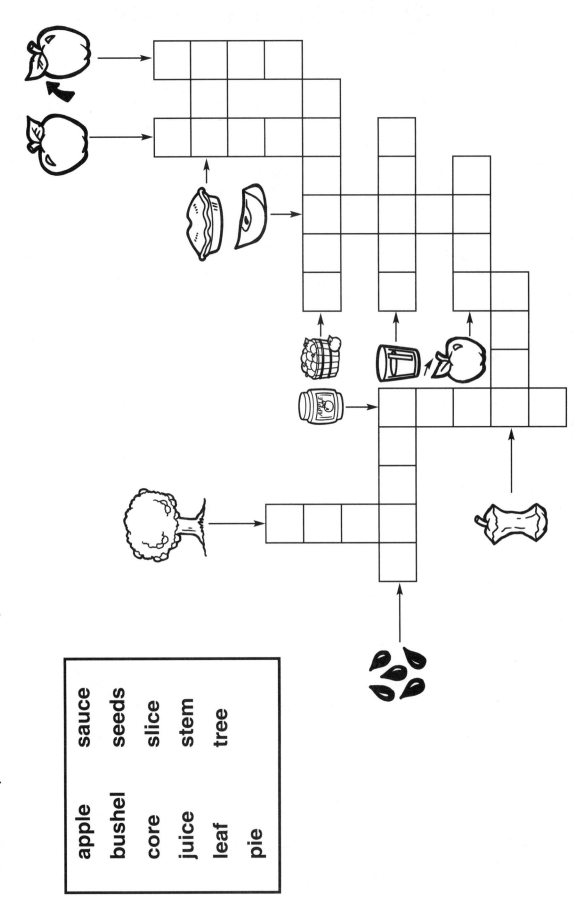

apple	sauce
bushel	seeds
core	slice
juice	stem
leaf	tree
pie	

Foods Made with Apples

Directions: Glue each word under the correct picture.

1.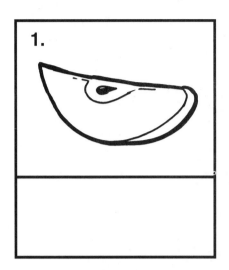

2.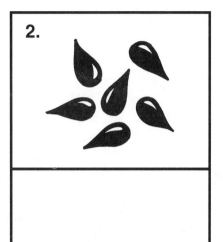

3.

4.

5.

6.

whole	juice
seeds	pie
sauce	slice

An Apple Tree

Directions: Write each word in the correct place on the diagram.

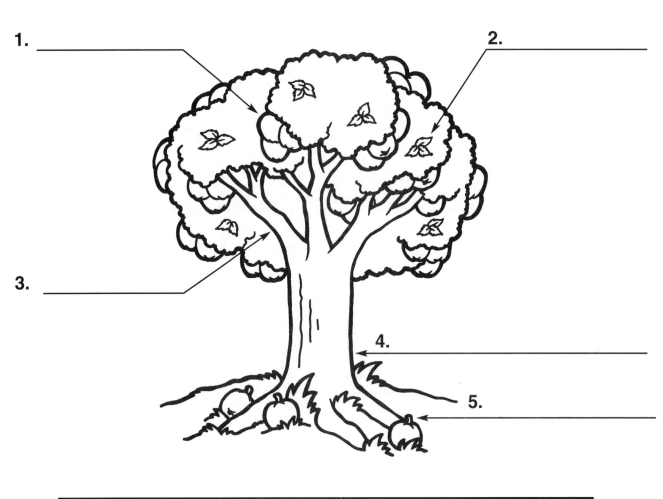

1. _____

2. _____

3. _____

4. _____

5. _____

| apple | branch | leaf | stem | trunk |

Directions: Write a sentence about the apple tree.

_____

_____

_____

_____

Bingo Boards

Card 1

Apple Bingo

pie	basket	half
slice	Free Space	core
tree	seeds	candy

Card 2

Apple Bingo

juice	seeds	stem
basket	Free Space	half
candy	tree	pie

Card 3

Apple Bingo

stem	pie	candy
basket	Free Space	slice
sauce	tree	leaf

Card 4

Apple Bingo

core	slice	tree
pie	Free Space	basket
leaf	sauce	juice

Bingo Boards

Card 5

Apple Bingo

tree	seeds	half
candy	Free Space	sauce
core	juice	slice

Card 6

Apple Bingo

basket	juice	seeds
tree	Free Space	core
half	pie	candy

Card 7

Apple Bingo

half	core	basket
juice	Free Space	leaf
stem	slice	sauce

Card 8

Apple Bingo

slice	candy	leaf
seeds	Free Space	half
stem	core	sauce

Bingo Calling Cards

pie	tree	core
basket	juice	candy apple
slice	seeds	sauce
half	leaf	stem

The Apple Game

	slice
	seeds
	leaf
	stem
	half
	core

Apple Dice

Assembly Instructions

1. Cut along all solid lines (including in and around large tabs).
2. Fold along all dashed lines.
3. Glue tab A to inside edge of Side D.
4. Fold in top and bottom flaps.

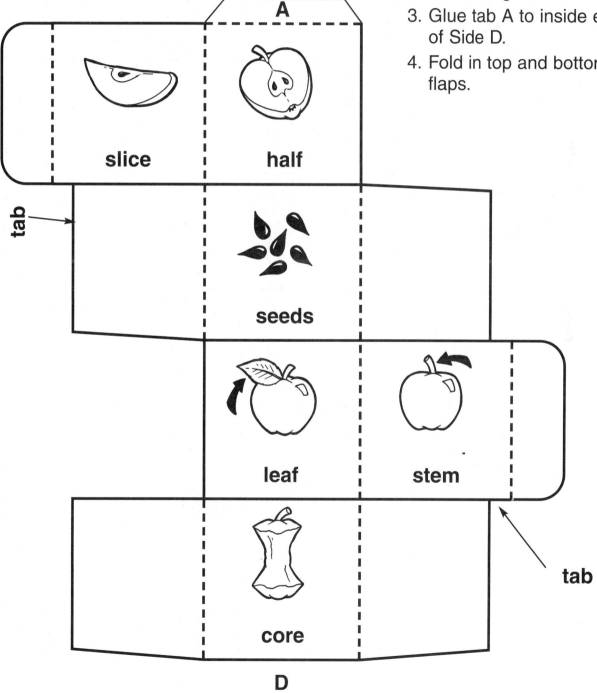

Apple History

Apple trees have been grown for thousands of years. In 1630, settlers brought apple seeds with them when they came to the New World.

In 1796, John McIntosh found 20 apple seeds. He planted them by his home. The apples were red. He called them McIntosh Red.

There are more than 100 kinds of apples. They can be red, yellow, or green. The inside of an apple can be white, yellow, or cream colored. Some apples are sweet. Some apples are tart.

Directions: Answer the questions.

1. What color can an apple be?

brown   blue   green
○   ○   ○

2. How many kinds of apples are there?

more than 100   about 10   more than 1,000
○   ○   ○

3. When were apple seeds brought to the New World?

1063   1360   1630
○   ○   ○

4. What did John McIntosh name the apples?

McIntosh Red   McIntosh Yellow   McIntosh Green
○   ○   ○

Johnny Appleseed

Johnny Appleseed's real name was John Chapman. He was born on September 26, 1776, in Massachusetts. John loved all people, animals, and nature. John was a vegetarian. A vegetarian is a person who does not eat meat.

John wore clothes made from potato sacks. He wore a tin pot on his head. He used the pot for cooking. John walked barefoot!

For more than 50 years John traveled throughout Ohio planting apple seeds and starting apple orchards. That is how he became known as Johnny Appleseed.

Johnny Appleseed died in March 1845.

Directions: Answer the questions.

1. What does a vegetarian eat?

meat   fruits and vegetables   grass
○   ○   ○

2. What was Johnny Appleseed's real name?

John Chapman   Johnny Apple   John Chaps
○   ○   ○

3. How many years did Johnny Appleseed plant apple seeds?

more than 100 years   more than 50 years   more than 25 years
○   ○   ○

4. What kind of hat did Johnny Appleseed wear?

a raccoon hat   a baseball cap   a tin pot
○   ○   ○

Favorite Flavor of Apples

Directions: Read each clue. If the answer is "yes," make an **O** in the box. If the answer is "no," make an **X** in the box.

	Green	Red	Yellow
Ben			
Dan			
Pam			

CLUES

- Ben eats green apples.

- Pam does not eat yellow apples.

1. Ben eats _____ apples.

2. Dan eats _____ apples.

3. Pam eats _____ apples.

The Real Apple

Directions: Read the clues. Cross off the pictures that do not fit the clues.

Hercules	Happy	Muscles
Nervy	Skip	Nosey
Puckers	Smiley	Puppet

CLUES

- I have been picked.
- I am smiling.
- I am a whole apple.
- I am exercising.
- I don't have a leaf.

Which apple am I? _____

Directions: Write another clue that would fit the mystery apple.

_____

- -

_____

Plenty of Apples

Directions: Use the graph to answer the questions.

1. How many apples shown with seeds are in the circle?

   _____

2. How many apples with stems are in the square?

   _____

3. How many apples shown with seeds are in <u>both</u> the circle and the square?

   _____

4. How many apples with leaves are in <u>both</u> the circle and the square?

   _____

5. How many apples with stems are in <u>only</u> the square?

   _____

Apple Sales

Directions: Use the pictures to create a graph.

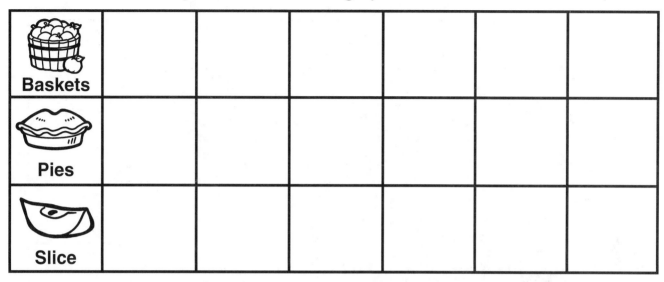

Baskets						
Pies						
Slice						

1. Were there more  or more sold?

2. Were there more or more sold?

3. Which way were the fewest apples sold?

4. What is your favorite way to eat apples?

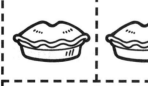  

How Tall Is Each Tree?

Directions: Measure the height of each tree to the nearest apple.

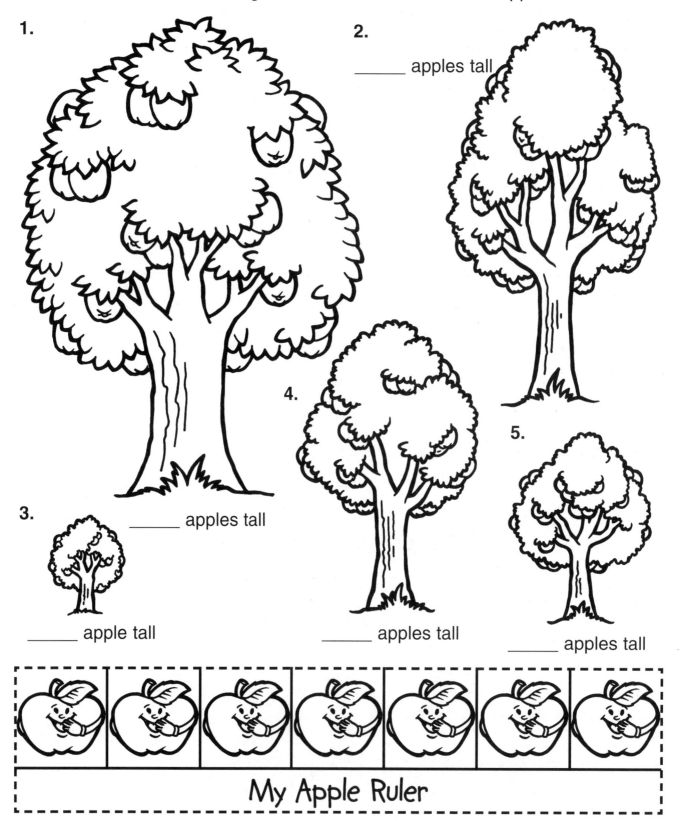

1.

2. _____ apples tall

4.

3. _____ apples tall

_____ apple tall

_____ apples tall

5. _____ apples tall

My Apple Ruler

September Calendar

Directions

- Photocopy the blank calendar (page 104) and the calendar "fill-ins" (page 103). (*Note:* Make a clean copy of the calendar fill-in page first and add any special school or local events. The students' names can be added to the birthday squares.)
- Have the students add the month and the days of the week to the calendar. (The students can also write the current year next to the name of the month.) Have the students write the calendar numbers in each square and add the special squares to the appropriate dates on the calendar.
- Using markers or crayons, have the students color the calendar and answer the questions about the calendars.

  (*Optional Step:* Fold a 12" x 18" inch piece of colored construction paper in half which is 12" x 9". Have the students open the folded piece of construction paper and glue or staple the completed calendar to the bottom half of the paper. On the top half have the students draw a picture.)

Calendar "Fill-ins"

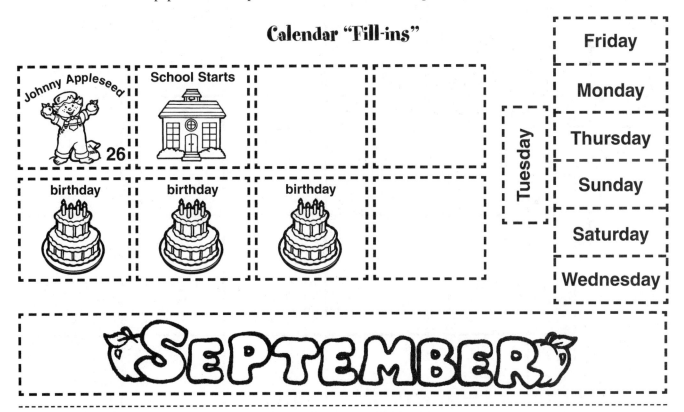

Calendar Questions

1. What is the name of the month?

   _____

2. What is the year? _____

3. How many days are in the month?

   _____

4. On what day does the month begin?

   _____

5. On what day does the month end?

   _____

6. How many days are in one week?

   _____

7. How many Saturdays are in the month?

   _____

8. How many birthdays are there?

   _____

Apple Smiles

Directions: Cut the pieces at the bottom of the page. Glue each puzzle piece in the correct space on the graph.

	1	2	3
A			
B			

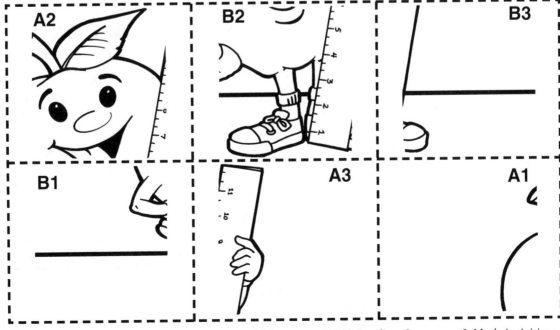

Apple Sort

Directions: Cut out the apple squares. Use the apple mat to find different ways the apples can be sorted.

Apple Sort

To be in this family _____.

Apple Patterns

Directions: Photocopy a class set of this page onto white construction paper. Have the students color and cut out the squares and arrange the squares into different patterns. Glue the squares onto a 12" long sentence strip.

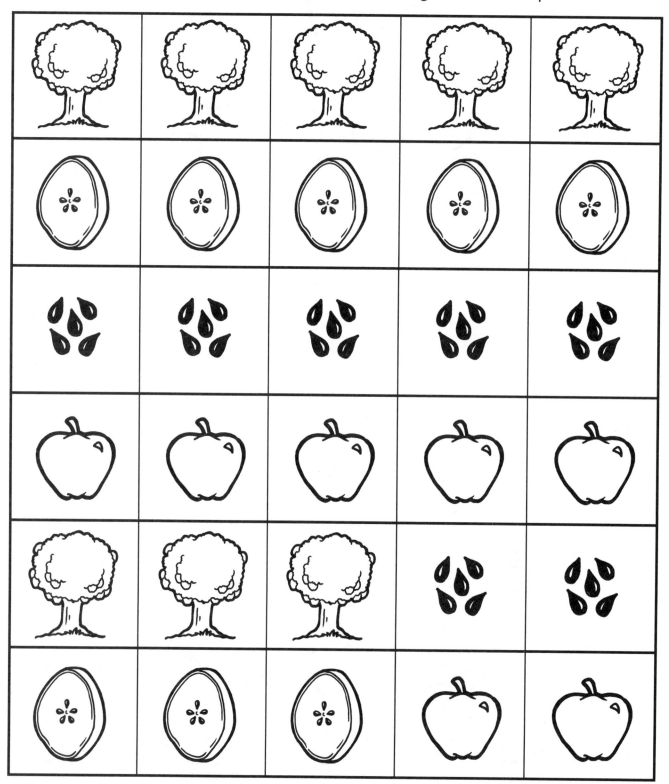

Apple Patterns

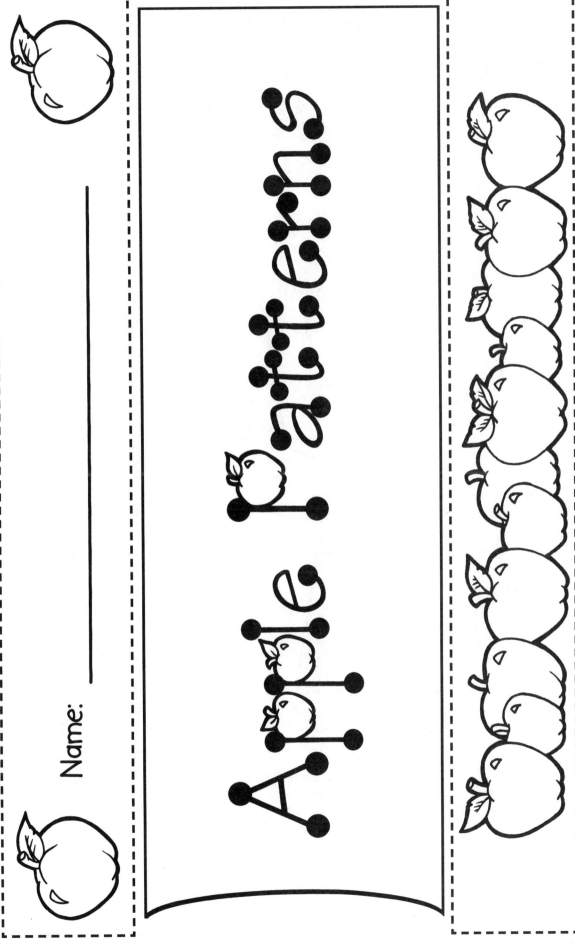

Name: _____

Apple Patterns

Apple Puzzle

Directions: Cut out the puzzle pieces and put them back together to make a picture.

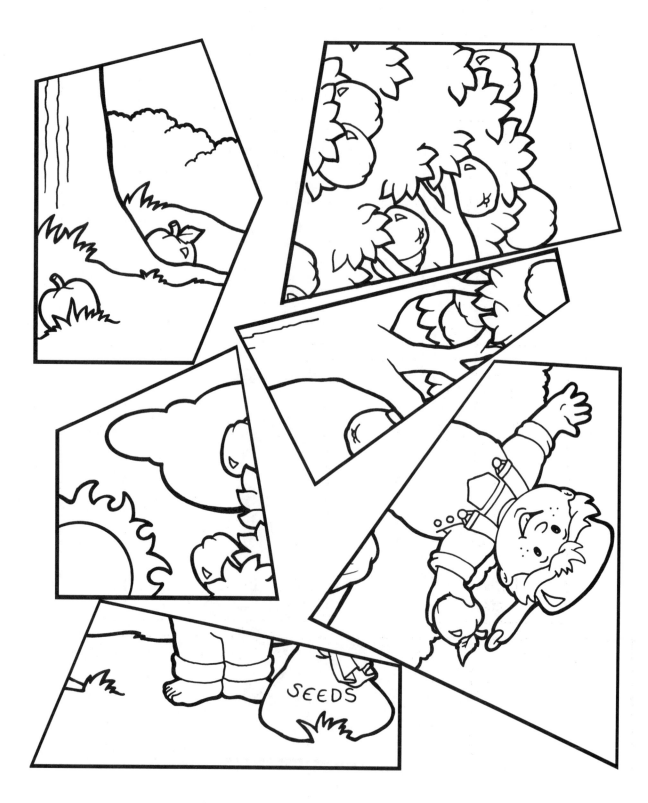

Draw the Apple Tree

Directions: Each item must be drawn consecutively starting with the number 1. Roll the die. If the number showing is a 1, go ahead and make the tree trunk. On your next turn, you must roll a 2 before drawing the leaves. If the number showing is not a 1, play continues with the next player. The first player to draw a complete apple tree, wins the game!

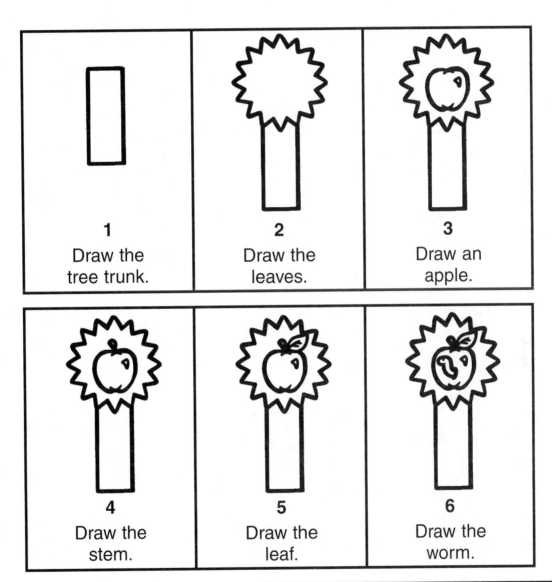

| **1** Draw the tree trunk. | **2** Draw the leaves. | **3** Draw an apple. |
| **4** Draw the stem. | **5** Draw the leaf. | **6** Draw the worm. |

Game 1	Game 2	Game 3	Game 4

Apple Halves

Directions: Cut out the apple halves at the bottom of the page. Match each number word to its correct number at the top.

Directions: Write the number word for each number.

8 _____   4 _____   7 _____   2 _____

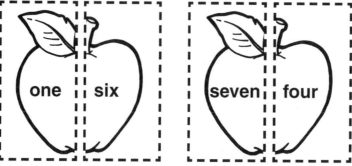

| three | ten | | nine | two | | five | eight |

| one | six | | seven | four |

Counting Apple Seeds

Directions: Count the number of seeds. Write the number on the line.

_____

_____

Are They Symmetrical?

Directions: Look at each picture. Circle "yes" if it is symmetrical and "no" if it is not symmetrical.

1. yes   no

2. yes   no

3. yes   no

4. yes   no

5. yes   no

6. yes   no

7. yes   no

8. yes   no

9. yes   no

10. yes   no

11. yes   no

12. yes   no

Johnny Appleseed Game

8			6/_	7	9/_	10	6/_
10			9/_	8			7
7							

Apple Seeds

START

Directions

- Place your marker on the apple seeds.
- Take the card from the top of the stack, read the number word, and move to the matching space.
- If you land on a space by the ladder, go down the slide to the space below it.

- If you land in the same space as another player, the other player has to move his or her counter back to the beginning of the game!
- The first player to land on the space next to the apple tree wins the game!

FINISH

9/_	8	7/_	6/_		10	9/_	9/_

Johnny Appleseed Game

Directions: Photocopy the cards and game markers onto cardstock or construction paper, laminate, cut apart, and store the pieces in a small, plastic bag.

Cards

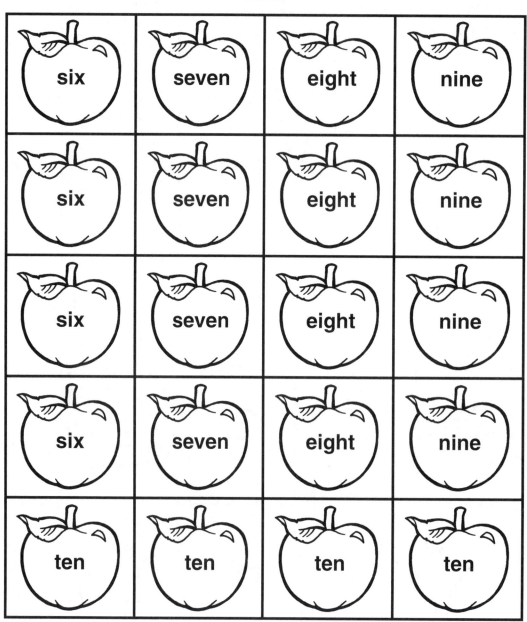

Game Markers

Apple Fractions

Cards

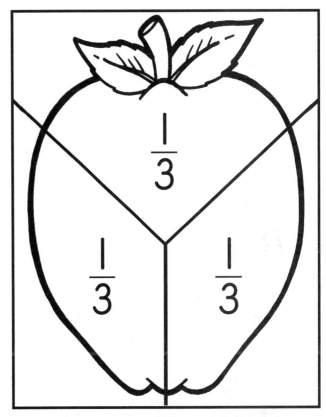

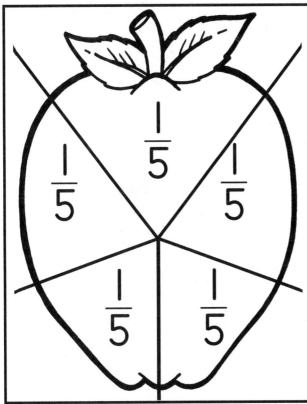

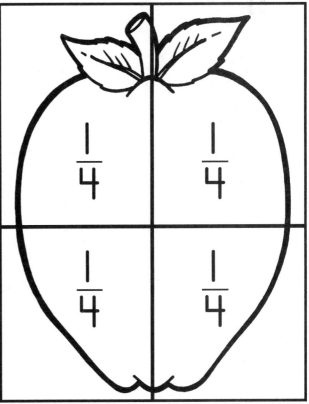

Apple Fractions

Spinner

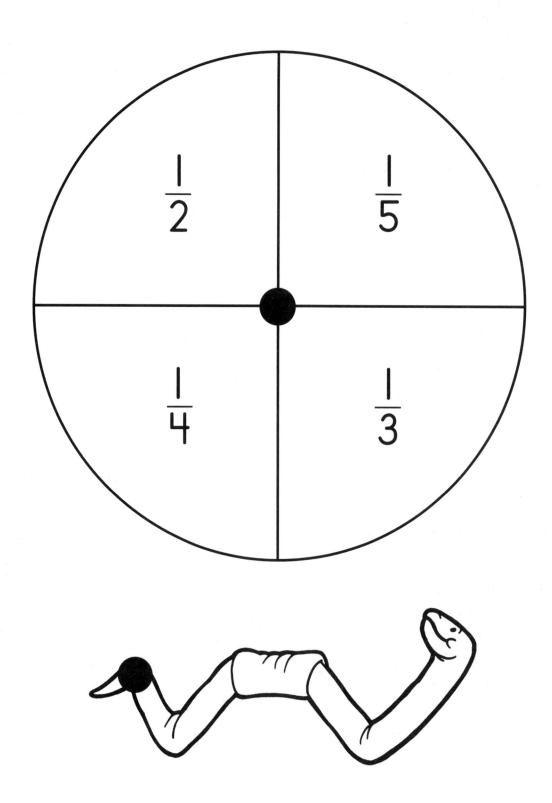

Four Apples in a Row

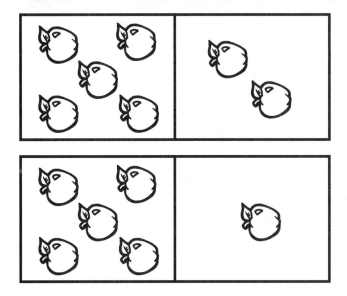

Directions

To Play: Taking turns, each player turns over a domino, counts the number of apples, and places an apple on the matching number on his or her playing board. The first player to get four apples in a row (vertically, horizontally, or diagonally) wins the game.

Variation #1: Give each player a blank apple. Have the student fill in the boxes using the numbers 6, 7, 8, 9, and 10.

Variation #2: Give each player a blank apple. Have the student write a different addition or subtraction problem that equals 6, 7, 8, 9, or 10 in each space.

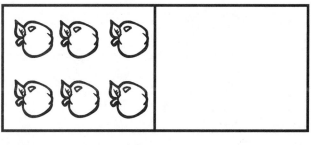

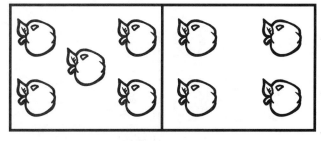

Four Apples in a Row

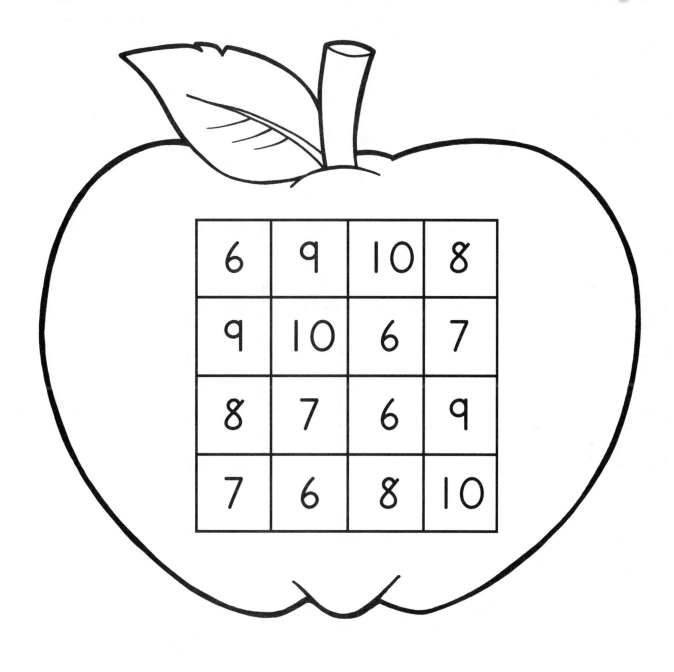

6	9	10	8
9	10	6	7
8	7	6	9
7	6	8	10

Four Apples in a Row

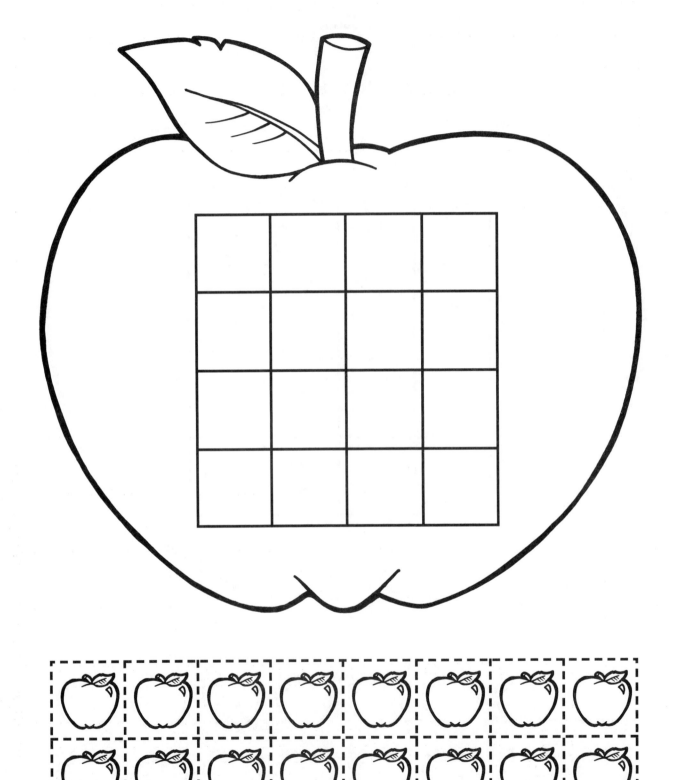

Favorite Color of Apples

Directions: Make a graph showing each student's favorite color of apple.

	Red	Yellow	Green
12			
11			
10			
9			
8			
7			
6			
5			
4			
3			
2			
1			

Apple Tasting Chart

Kind of Apple	Color	Size	Taste

Answer Key

Page 75

Facts: Apples have seeds. There are many kinds of apples. Apples grow on trees.

Opinions: Green apples are my favorite. Apples are delicious. I like apples.

Statements will vary.

Page 76

Apples: healthy snack, covered with skin, comes with a stem

Candied Apples: special treat, covered in caramel, comes on a stick

Page 77

1. apples
2. core
3. half
4. seeds
5. tree

Page 79

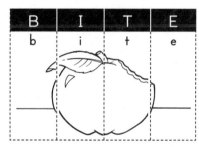

Page 80

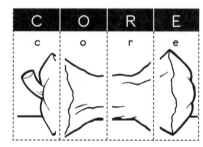

Page 81

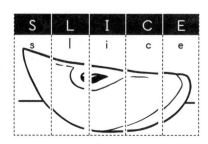

Page 82

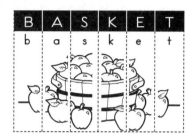

Page 87

Page 88

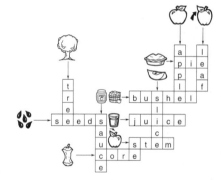

Page 89

1. slice
2. seeds
3. whole
4. pie
5. sauce
6. juice

Page 90

1. apple
2. leaf
3. branch
4. trunk
5. stem

Answers will vary for sentence.

Page 96

1. green
2. more than 100
3. 1630
4. McIntosh Red

Page 97

1. fruits and vegetables
2. John Chapman
3. more than 50 years
4. a tin pot

Answer Key

Page 98

		Green	Red	Yellow
Ben		O	X	X
Dan		X	X	O
Pam		X	O	X

1. green   2. yellow   3. red

Page 99

Skip

Page 100

1. 3   2. 9   3. 3   4. 0   5. 5

Page 101

Baskets						
Pies						
Slice						

1. The picture of the pie should be circled.
2. The picture of the basket of apples should be circled.
3. The picture of the slice of apple should be circled.
4. Answers will vary.

Page 102

1. 5   2. 4   3. 1   4. 3   5. 2

Page 105

Page 110

Page 112

8 = eight, 4 = four, 7 = seven, 2 = two

Page 113

4, 9, 1, 3
6, 2, 5, 8
7, 0

Page 114

1. no	5. no	9. yes
2. yes	6. yes	10. yes
3. no	7. no	11. no
4. no	8. yes	12. no

October

Table of Contents

October

Introduction

October contains activities and games that cover monthly themes and events. The students will learn basic information about important October events. Through a variety of games and activities, the students will be able to practice important skills covered in the primary grades.

Reading and Language Activities

- **October Cover (page 131):** Simply photocopy the pages the students are to do and use this page as the cover for this unit. Or, photocopy sets of the writing paper (pages 6–8) for each student and staple to make a writing packet. The October Cover can be used as the cover for the writing packet.

- **Check-Off List (page 10):** This can be used to keep track of each activity as it is completed by the student.

- **October Writing Prompts (pages 132 and 133):** Writing prompts for each one of the four domains are provided. The writing prompts are a fun way to explore October happenings!

- **Christopher Columbus (page 134), Spiders and Insects (page 135),** and **Halloween (page 136):** These pages are cut-and-paste activities that have the students sort statements into different categories.

- **It Happens in October (page 137):** Students are sure to enjoy placing October vocabulary in the correct alphabetical order.

- **How to Grow a Pumpkin (page 138):** Students will learn how to grow a pumpkin doing this activity. Pages can be cut apart and then stapled to make a mini-booklet.

- **Letter Matches (pages 139–142):** These cut-and-paste activities reinforce identifying and matching uppercase and lowercase letters. The students cut out the "puzzle pieces" at the bottom of the page and glue them in place under the matching uppercase letter. If done correctly, the letters will spell a word and a picture will be revealed.

- **Making Statements and Questions (page 143):** This activity page contains rebus-like pictures and high-frequency words. The students cut apart the words and pictures and arrange and rearrange the words and pictures to make different questions and statements. When doing this activity with the whole class, an overhead transparency of the page can be made or use a photocopy machine to enlarge the words and pictures so that they can be easily seen by all of the students. Sample sentences that can be made are as follows:

I see a spider.	A bat is by the scarecrow.
Where is the pumpkin?	The pumpkin is under a fence.
We see the bat.	The pumpkin is on a fence.

- **How Many Words Can You Make? (page 144):** This activity is similar to "making words." The students cut apart the letter cards and arrange and rearrange the letters to make different words. When doing this activity with the whole class, make an overhead transparency of the page. Call on individual students to use the overhead to show the class a word he or she has made. This is also a great activity to send home as homework with the students. Sample words that can be made are as follows:

  Two Letters: Al, he, me, no
  Three Letters: Hal, Lee, owl, low, how, now, won, one, eel, all, hen, owe
  Four Letters: when, wall, halo, well, lone, lean, heel, heal, hale, hole, hall, Owen
  Five+ Letters: wheel, whale

October

Reading and Language Activities *(cont.)*

- **The Pumpkins (pages 145 and 146):** This rebus story activity uses pictures and high-frequency words to tell a story. The students can feel successful when they are able to read the story with little or no help from the teacher! This is also a great story to send home with the students.

  The story reads: *The kids went to the pumpkin patch. The girl saw a big pumpkin. The boy saw a small pumpkin. The kids paid for the pumpkins. The kids put the pumpkins in the wagon and took the pumpkins home. At home, the kids cut the tops off. The kids dug out the seeds. The kids carved faces on the pumpkins. The kids put candles into the jack-o-lanterns. Boo!*

- **Halloween Word Search (page 147)** and **Kids in Costumes (page 148):** Students will find vocabulary words about Halloween in a word search or a crossword puzzle.

- **On Halloween (page 149)** and **Parts of a Pumpkin (page 150):** In these activities, students will place labels underneath a picture or write the words on a diagram.

- **Halloween Bingo (pages 151–153):** This game provides eight different bingo cards and matching calling cards. Halloween Bingo reinforces vocabulary and language development skills in a fun-filled, non-threatening manner.

- **Halloween Antonyms (pages 154 and 155):** This activity introduces the concept of antonyms (opposites) in a concrete manner. The Halloween Antonym activities can be placed at a center or sent home as homework. The Halloween Antonym cards (page 154) can be used with the whole class, small groups, or with a partner. Photocopy, color, and laminate two sets of cards for every 2–3 students. The cards can be used in a variety of ways.

  Concentration: Lay two sets of cards face down on the table. Taking turns, each student turns over two cards. If the cards match (are antonyms for each other), the student keeps both cards and takes another turn. If the cards do not match, the student returns both cards to their original places. The student with the most matches wins the game.

  Go Fish: Shuffle two sets of cards and deal five cards to each student. Each student looks at his or her cards and removes any matches (cards that are antonyms for each other). Taking turns, the student asks the player on his or her left, "Do you have the card that is the opposite of . . . (name the antonym)?" If the player has the card, he or she gives it to the student. If not, the player says, "Sorry! Go fish!" Then the student needs to take the top card from the cards not dealt. The student with the most matches wins the game.

- **Christopher Columbus (page 156), Day of the Dead (page 157), Why Do Leaves Change Color? (page 158), Pumpkins (page 159), Owls (page 160), Arachnids (page 161),** and **Bats (page 162):** These pages provide background information on the topics, as well as several comprehension questions for the students to answer.

Math Activities

- **Halloween Costumes (page 163):** This is a logic activity. Once a clue fits a person, place an O in the correct box and Xs in the rest of the boxes in that same row and column. Through the process of elimination, the logic problem can be solved!

- **Trick-or-Treat! (page 164):** This is a logic activity. As each clue is read, the students cross off the pictures that meet (or do not meet) the clue.

October

Math Activities *(cont.)*

- **Costume Parade (page 165)** and **Candy Sort (page 166):** In these activities, students work with charts and graphs and answer questions about them.

- **Costumes for Sale (page 167):** Students will enjoy identifying the cost of each costume in this activity.

- **October Calendar (pages 168):** Students will put together all the different parts of a calendar using page 168 and page 104. Then students will answer some questions about it.

- **On Halloween Night (page 169):** Students will glue all the pieces of the puzzle in the correct place on the graph to form a picture.

- **Pumpkin Sort (pages 170 and 171):** This activity can be done with the whole class. Make an overhead transparency of both pages. Place the large pumpkin transparency (page 171) on the overhead projector. Place several of the pumpkin pictures inside the pumpkin and the remaining pictures outside the pumpkin. Ask the students, "What is the rule to be in this family?" Call on students to answer.

  Suggested ways to sort the pumpkins are as follows:

  Pumpkins with/without candles   Pumpkins and jack-o-lanterns
  Pumpkins with/without stems   Pumpkins with/without leaves
  Pumpkins with/without tops.

  To extend this activity, provide each student with copies of both pages and them sort the pumpkins and write the rule on the back of the page. Take a few minutes each day to share several of the sortings with the students and see if they can discover the rules!

- **Costumes on Parade (pages 172 and 173):** Students will make patterns using different Halloween costumes. Photocopy the pattern sleeve onto construction paper, fold on the dashed lines, and glue (or tape) the back to create the pattern sleeve. For each student provide three to four 12" lengths of sentence strips, a pattern sleeve, and a photocopy of the pictures. Have the students use the pictures to create patterns on the sentence strips.

- **Bat Facts (pages 174–177):** Each pair of students will need the Bat Facts page, the spinners, and both dice to play the game. Taking turns, each student rolls the dice and writes each number on the ears and the total on the bat's face. One student spins the spinner. The student who has the sum that corresponds to the spinner, colors the bat and wins the first round. Both students then move on to the next bat on their pages and repeat the above steps.

- **Number Match (pages 178–181):** This activity reinforces numbers, number words, and counting items to 10.

- **The Haunted House Game (pages 182–184):** This game can be used to reinforce addition to 6, subtraction to 6, and mixed practice. For each group (two to four students), provide a game board and a copy of the math problems for the student to use. Taking turns, each student turns over the top card, solves the problem, and moves his or her marker to the nearest space with the answer. If another student lands in a space already occupied by a player, the first player gets bumped back to start. If a student lands on a space next to a spider web, the student can "climb across" the web (it is a short cut) to the next row of numbers. The first student to each the haunted house wins the game.

- **Spider Man (pages 185 and 186):** In this activity, students use dice to record math problems on a spider.

October Writing Prompts

Domain	Writing Prompt	Word Bank
Practical/Informative	How to Carve a Jack-o-Lantern	candle, carve, design, face, knife, patch, pick, pulp, pumpkin, seeds
Practical/Informative	Christopher Columbus	America, Indies, Nina, October 12, 1492, Pinta, Santa Maria, Spain
Practical/Informative	A Nocturnal Animal	burrow, den, eyesight, hearing, hunts, nighttime, quiet, safe
Practical/Informative	Spiders	arachnid, black, legs, silky, spinning, strong, webs
Practical/Informative	Owls	birds of prey, carnivores, eyesight, feathers, hearing
Analytical/Expository	Would a bat make a good pet?	eat, fly, good hearing, insects, mammals, nocturnal
Analytical/Expository	Would you have liked to have sailed with Christopher Columbus?	adventure, fun, rough, sailing, scary, seasick, travel
Analytical/Expository	Should people be afraid of bats?	fangs, flying, fruit, hunters, insect, nocturnal, wings

October Writing Prompts

Domain	Writing Prompt	Word Bank
Imaginative/Narrative	A Very Scary Story	With the students, brainstorm a list of scary events and scary words.
Imaginative/Narrative	What should you do if you meet a mummy?	become friends, run, say "Hello," scream, unravel, unwrap, yell
Imaginative/Narrative	Tell about a night spent in a haunted house.	broom, creaking, creatures, creepy, dark, haunted, noisy, scary, spooky, witch
Imaginative/Narrative	What would happen if your jack-o-lantern became alive?	candle, falling, floating, friendly, grinning, lumpy, orange, rolling, scary, spooky
Sensory/Descriptive	I'm a leaf.	autumn, change colors, fall, food, rest, sunshine, tree, water
Sensory/Descriptive	A Favorite Halloween Costume	beautiful, cartoon, character, funny, movie, scary, silly
Sensory/Descriptive	The Perfect Pumpkin	big, bumpy, just right, lumpy, oval, rough, round, small, smooth
Sensory/Descriptive	A Favorite Halloween Candy	chewy, chocolate, colors, hard, rough, round, smooth, sour, sticky, sweet

Christopher Columbus

Directions: Cut out the small boxes at the bottom of the page. Glue the statements in the correct box below.

Then	Now

Directions: Write another true statement about Columbus' ship.

_____

_____

_____

Took bread, meat, and water	Was a tough and scary voyage
Sailed on three small ships	Has a large kitchen with lots of different foods
Enjoyed the journey and the scenery	Has one large ship with an engine

Spiders and Insects

Directions: Cut out the small boxes at the bottom of the page. Glue the statements in the correct box below.

Spiders	Insects

Directions: Write another true statement about spiders or insects.

_____

_____

_____

six legs	three body parts
can go a year or more without eating	eight legs
two body parts	has two antennas and might have wings

Halloween

Directions: Cut out the small boxes at the bottom of the page. Glue the statements in the correct box below.

Facts	Opinions

Directions: Write a factual statement about Halloween.

_____

- -

_____

_____

- -

_____

Some costumes are scary.	Halloween is the best holiday!
Halloween is fun.	Some people go trick-or-treating.
Halloween is on October 31st.	Pumpkins are a symbol of Halloween.

It Happens in October

Directions: Cut out and glue the picture and word cards in alphabetical order.

1.

2.

3.

4.

5.

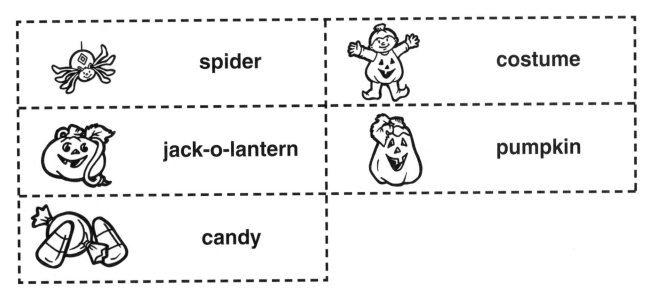

spider

costume

jack-o-lantern

pumpkin

candy

3

The seed sprouts and becomes a plant.

6

The pumpkin is carved and becomes a jack-o-lantern.

2

Dig a hole and plant the seed. Water the seed.

5

The flower grows and becomes a pumpkin.

How to Grow a Pumpkin

1

Name: _____

4

The plant grows and becomes a flower.

Letter Match

Directions: Cut out the boxes at the bottom of the page. Glue the lowercase letter box to the uppercase letter box to find a picture.

B	A	T	S

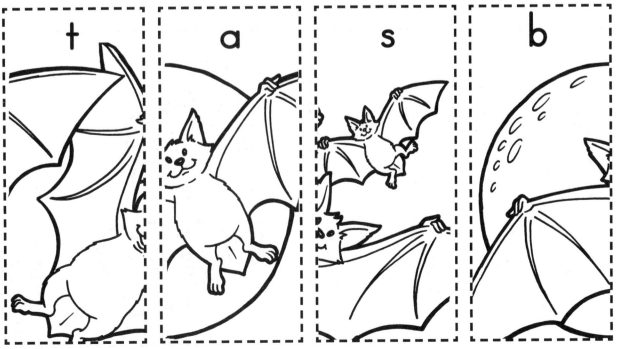

t   a   s   b

Letter Match

Directions: Cut out the boxes at the bottom of the page. Glue the lowercase letter box to the uppercase letter box to find a picture.

G	H	O	S	T

Letter Match

Directions: Cut out the boxes at the bottom of the page. Glue the lowercase letter box to the uppercase letter box to find a picture.

S	P	I	D	E	R

d e i p r s

Letter Match

Directions: Cut out the boxes at the bottom of the page. Glue the lowercase letter box to the uppercase letter box to find a picture.

C	O	S	T	U	M	E

c   e   m   o   s   u   t

Making Questions and Statements

p	I	.	¿
tree	see	by	on
fence	The / under	is	the
pumpkin	bat	Where	What
spider	scarecrow		We

How Many Words Can You Make?

Directions: Cut out the letters at the bottom of the page. Rearrange the letters to make different words. Write each word under the correct heading.

2-Letter Words	3-Letter Words	4-Letter Words	5-or-More Letter Words

H A L L O W E E N

The Pumpkins

The   kids   went to the pumpkin patch.   The   girl

saw a big   pumpkin.   The   boy   saw a small pumpkin.

The   kids   paid for the   pumpkins.

The   kids   put the   pumpkins   in the wagon

and took the pumpkins   home.

At   home,   the   kids   cut   the

tops   off. The   kids   dug out the   seeds.

The   kids   carved   faces   on the   pumpkins.

The   kids   put   candles into the   jack-o-lanterns.

Boo!

Boo!

Halloween Word Search

Directions: Find and color each word.

H	A	L	L	O	W	E	E	N	A	B	C	D	E
Q	P	R	S	W	I	T	C	H	E	S	P	P	F
G	O	T	U	L	A	B	M	O	O	N	O	O	G
H	B	A	T	S	C	E	S	F	M	L	K	K	C
O	T	R	I	C	K	O	R	T	R	E	A	T	A
S	N	V	X	W	Y	D	P	U	M	S	K	I	N
T	M	H	O	U	S	E	S	M	G	H	I	J	D
S	P	I	D	E	R	S	L	E	K	J	I	H	Y

PUMPKIN	MOON	SPIDERS	HOUSES
COSTUME	OWLS	CANDY	TRICK OR TREAT
HALLOWEEN	BATS	GHOSTS	WITCHES

Kids in Costumes

Directions: Complete the crossword puzzle.

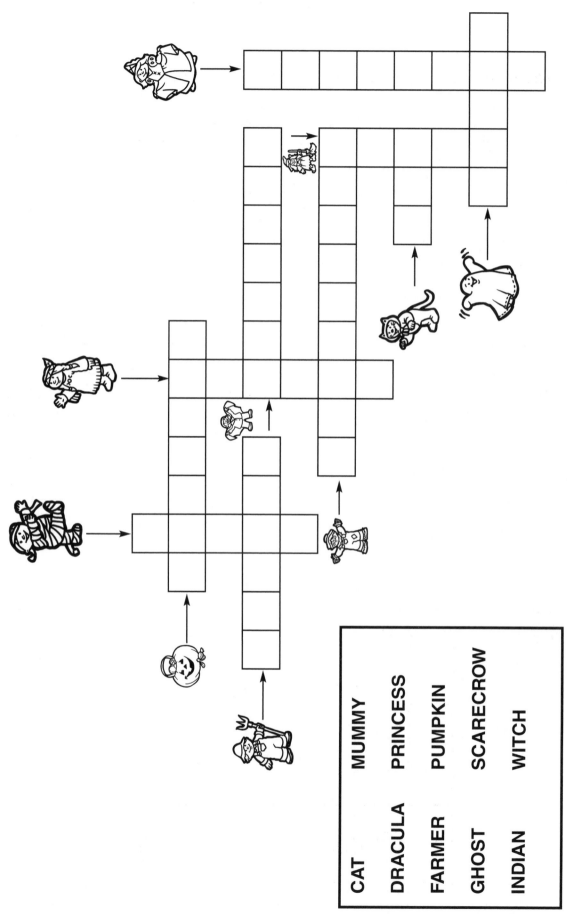

CAT	MUMMY
DRACULA	PRINCESS
FARMER	PUMPKIN
GHOST	SCARECROW
INDIAN	WITCH

On Halloween

Directions: Glue each word under the correct picture.

1. 	2. 	3. 
4. 	5. 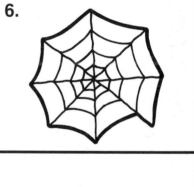	6. 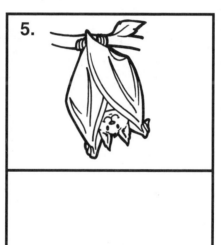

bat	ghost
candy corn	jack-o-lantern
Dracula	web

Parts of a Pumpkin

Directions: Label each part of the pumpkin.

face	pumpkin	seeds	stem	top	vine

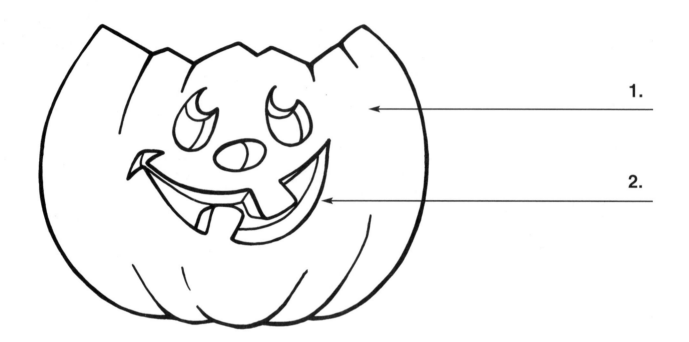

1. _____

2. _____

3. _____

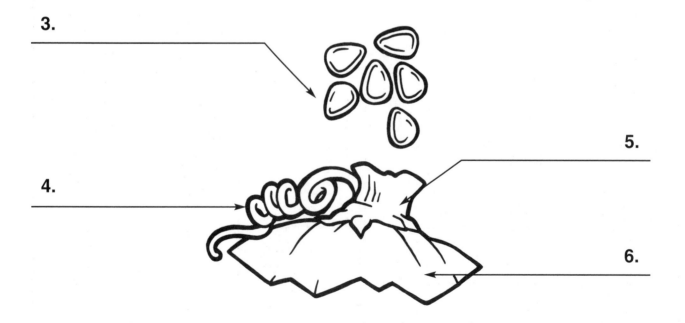

4. _____

5. _____

6. _____

Bingo Cards

Card 1

Halloween Bingo

Dracula	mummy	cat
Frankenstein	Free Space	scarecrow
fairy	clown	ghost

Card 2

Halloween Bingo

clown	pumpkin	witch
doll	Free Space	cat
Frankenstein	Dracula	fairy

Card 3

Halloween Bingo

pumpkin	ghost	scarecrow
Dracula	Free Space	wizard
witch	fairy	doll

Card 4

Halloween Bingo

ghost	clown	pumpkin
scarecrow	Free Space	doll
mummy	Frankenstein	wizard

Bingo Cards

Card 5

Halloween Bingo

wizard	Frankenstein	cat
clown	Free Space	mummy
scarecrow	ghost	fairy

Card 6

Halloween Bingo

witch	cat	Dracula
wizard	Free Space	scarecrow
mummy	clown	Frankenstein

Card 7

Halloween Bingo

Dracula	witch	cat
doll	Free Space	wizard
pumpkin	fairy	mummy

Card 8

Halloween Bingo

pumpkin	ghost	witch
clown	Free Space	scarecrow
wizard	Frankenstein	doll

Bingo Calling Cards

Dracula	ghost	doll
witch	mummy	wizard
Frankenstein	clown	cat
fairy	scarecrow	pumpkin

Halloween Antonyms

Directions: Cut out the pictures. Match each picture to its antonym.

black	white	happy
over	under	pumpkin
full	empty	asleep
awake	mad	jack-o-lantern

Halloween Antonyms

Directions: Cut out the pictures. Match each picture to its antonym.

1.
over

4.
black

2.
awake

5.
jack-o-lantern

3.
empty

6.
happy

white   under   asleep

mad   full   pumpkin

Christopher Columbus

Christopher Columbus was an explorer. In 1492, King Ferdinand II and Queen Isabella of Spain provided three ships to Columbus. The three ships were the Nina, the Pinta, and the Santa Maria.

Columbus was supposed to find a faster route to the far east (Asia) in order to trade for valuable spices. Instead, on October 12, 1492, after five weeks of sailing, Columbus landed in the New World.

Today, Christopher Columbus day is celebrated on the second Monday in October.

Directions: Answer the questions. Fill in the circle with the correct answer.

1. When did Columbus land in America?

October 12, 1492   October 12, 1992   October 12, 1692
    ◯   ◯   ◯

2. How many ships did Columbus have?

1   2   3
◯   ◯   ◯

3. Who gave the ships to Columbus?

king and queen of Spain   king and queen of Italy
    ◯   ◯

4. What did the King and Queen want to trade?

gold   spices   jewels
◯   ◯   ◯

Day of the Dead

Dia de los Muertos or Day of the Dead, is a way of honoring and remembering the dead. This month-long ritual is more than 3,000 years old. The Aztecs used skulls to symbolize death and rebirth. They believed that during this month their relatives would return and visit them.

Today, people living in Mexico, South America, and parts of the United States still celebrate the Day of the Dead. Some people dance about wearing wooden skulls called **calacas**. Some people build altars in their homes. The altars are decorated with candles, pictures of loved ones, and food. Other people visit the cemetery and decorate their loved one's grave with candles, food, and toys.

Directions: Answer the questions. Fill in the circle with the correct answer.

1. Whom does Day of the Dead honor?

      dead relatives   skulls   Aztecs

           ◯   ◯   ◯

2. What are **calacas**?

      instruments   skulls   chocolate

           ◯   ◯   ◯

3. What do some people build?

      altars   boards   homes

           ◯   ◯   ◯

Why Do Leaves Change Color?

During the shorter length of sunlight during the winter months, leaves do not receive enough sunlight or water for photosynthesis to take place. Photosynthesis is how leaves make energy.

In the fall, the leaves start to "shut down" which means they make less carbon. When this happens, the bright green of the chlorophyll in the leaves disappears leaving behind leaves that are red, yellow, orange, or purple.

The tree will rest for the winter and will live off of the food that it has stored.

Directions: Answer the questions. Fill in the circle with the correct answer.

1. In which season do the leaves begin to change colors?

    winter   summer   fall

    ◯   ◯   ◯

2. What causes the leaves to change color?

    less carbon   more carbon   more chlorophyll

    ◯   ◯   ◯

3. How will the tree survive the winter?

    live off its stored food   grow more food   make more food

    ◯   ◯   ◯

4. What color will the leaves change?

    pink   red   gray

    ◯   ◯   ◯

Pumpkins

Pumpkins are fruits—not vegetables. Pumpkins, cucumbers, melons, squashes, and gourds are all members of the cucurbitaceae family.

All "giant" pumpkins grown today came from seeds developed by William Warnock around the turn of the century. He grew the very first, record-breaking pumpkin in 1893. The pumpkin weighed 365 pounds!

Directions: Answer the questions. Fill in the circle with the correct answer.

1. To which food group do pumpkins belong?

      fruits   vegetables   dairy

       ◯   ◯   ◯

2. What did William Warnock develop?

giant pumpkin seeds   giant tomato seeds   giant apple seeds

      ◯   ◯   ◯

3. How much did the first giant pumpkin weigh?

  563 pounds   365 pounds   635 pounds

      ◯   ◯   ◯

4. Which other food item is in the same family as the pumpkin?

   potatoes   oranges   melons

      ◯   ◯   ◯

Owls

Owls are nocturnal birds of prey. A bird of prey hunts for its food. Owls have excellent vision and hearing. An owl's wings allow it to swoop down to catch its prey. Owls eat rodents, insects, frogs, and birds.

Owls have large eyes that face forward. Because its eyes are so big, the owl can not move its eyes to see what is going on around it. Instead, the owl is able to turn its head almost all the way around.

There are 162 kinds of owls. The elf owl is the smallest owl. It is 6" long and weighs 1 1/2 ounces! The largest owl is the great gray owl. It is 33" long and weighs 3 pounds.

Directions: Answer the questions. Fill in the circle with the correct answer.

1. What kind of animal is an owl?

a reptile ◯ a mammal ◯ bird of prey ◯

2. What is an owl able to do?

turn its head ◯ move its eyes ◯ wiggle its eyes ◯

3. Which owl is the largest?

elf owl ◯ great gray owl ◯ barn owl ◯

4. What do birds of prey eat?

plants ◯ meat ◯ fruit ◯

Arachnids

Spiders are arachnids. Spiders have two body parts—a head and an abdomen—and eight legs. Spiders are cold blooded.

Spiders can be black, brown, white, gray, red, yellow, green, or orange. They can live just about anywhere on the earth. Most spiders can live for fifteen years without eating.

Arachnids and insects are not the same. Insects have three body parts (the head, thorax, and abdomen), two antennae, and six legs. Some insects also have wings.

Directions: Answer the questions. Fill in the circle with the correct answer.

1. How many legs does a spider have?

four   eight   six
○   ○   ○

2. How long can most spiders live without eating?

one year   fifteen years   hundred years
○   ○   ○

3. How many body parts does a spider have?

two   three   four
○   ○   ○

4. What is the scientific name for a spider?

creepy-crawly   insect   arachnid
○   ○   ○

Bats

There are over 900 kinds of bats. Bats are the only mammals that can fly. A bat's wings are actually long fingers covered with a thin layer of skin. Bats have weak legs and do not walk very well.

Like people, bats are born alive, have fur on their bodies, drink milk from their mothers, are warm blooded, and have lungs.

Bats are nocturnal. That means they are active during the night. During the day, bats sleep hanging upside down.

Bats can live just about anywhere in the world, except at the North and South Poles.

The smallest bat is the bumblebee bat. Its wingspan is only 6" long and it weighs less than a penny. The largest bat is the flying fox. It has a 6' wingspan and weighs two pounds.

Directions: Answer the questions. Fill in the circle with the correct answer.

1. Which bat is the smallest bat?

vampire bat ○   bumblebee bat ○   flying fox ○

2. Where can bats live?

just about anywhere ○   at the North Pole ○   at the South Pole ○

3. When do bats sleep?

never ○   at night ○   during the day ○

Halloween Costumes

Directions: Read each clue. If the answer is "yes," make an **O** in the box. If the answer is "no," make an **X** in the box.

	Scarecrow	Cat	Pumpkin
Cleo			
Stanley			
Tom			

CLUES

- Cleo dressed as a pumpkin.
- Tom did not wear the scarecrow costume.

Which costume did each person wear?

1. 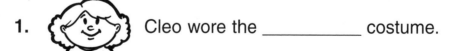 Cleo wore the _____ costume.

2. 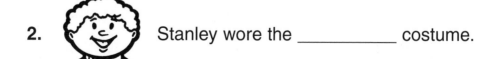 Stanley wore the _____ costume.

3. 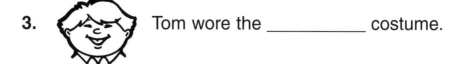 Tom wore the _____ costume.

Trick-or-Treat!

Directions: Read the clues and then cross off the pictures that do no fit the clues.

Whisper	Frank	Baggy
Cheery	Pumpkin	Kitty
Spooky	Captain	Wiz

CLUES

- I am not holding anything.
- I have two feet.
- I am not a plant, food, or an animal.

Who am I? _____

Directions: Write another clue that would fit the mystery person.

_____

_____

Costume Parade

Directions: Use the chart to answer the questions.

1. Write the number.

 _____   _____   _____   _____

2. How many clowns are in the circle?

_____

3. How many ghosts are in the square?

_____

4. How many ghosts are in <u>both</u> the circle and the square?

_____

5. How many cats are in the circle?

_____

6. Which costume is in both the circle and the square?

_____

Candy Sort

Directions: Cut out the candies at the bottom of the page and glue them to make the graph. Then answer the questions.

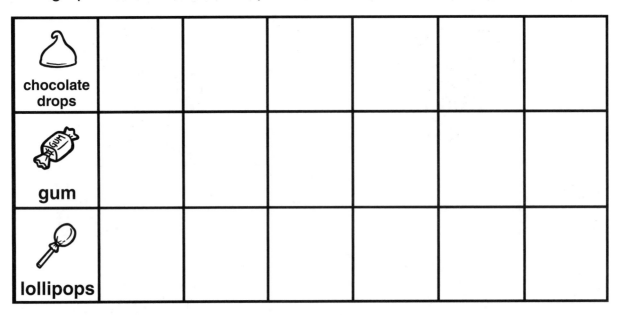

chocolate drops						
gum						
lollipops						

1. Write the number. _____   _____   _____

2. Are there more or more ?

3. Are there more or more ?

4. Are there more or more ?

5. How many candies are there in all? _____

Costumes for Sale

Directions: How much does each costume cost? Write in the amount.

1. _____ ¢

2. _____ ¢

3. _____ ¢

4. _____ ¢

5. _____ ¢

6. _____ ¢

October Calendar

Directions: Photocopy the blank calendar (page 104) and the calendar "fill-ins" on this page. (*Note:* Make a clean copy of the calendar fill-in page first and add any special school or local events. The students' names can be added to the birthday squares. Then photocopy the completed "fill-in" page.) Have the students add the month and the days of the week to the calendar. The students can also write the current year next to the name of the month.

Have the students write the calendar numbers in each square. Then have the students add the special squares to the appropriate dates on the calendar. Using markers or crayons, have the students color the calendar. Then have the students answer the questions about the calendars.

(*Optional Step:* Fold a 12" x 18" piece of colored construction paper in half. Have the students open the folded piece of construction paper and glue or staple the completed calendar to the bottom half of the paper. On the top half, have the students draw a picture for the current month.)

Calendar "Fill-ins"

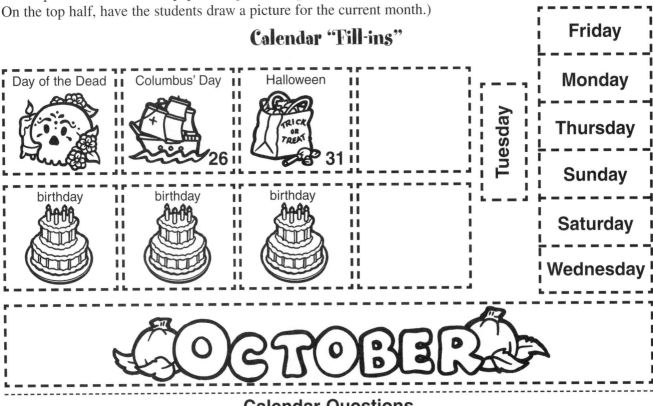

Calendar Questions

1. What is the name of the month? _____

2. What is the year? _____

3. How many days are in the month? _____

4. On what day does the month begin? _____

5. On what day does the month end? _____

6. How many Mondays are in the month? _____

7. How many birthdays are there? _____

8. Name a special event or holiday for this month. _____

On Halloween Night

Directions: Glue each puzzle piece in the correct space.

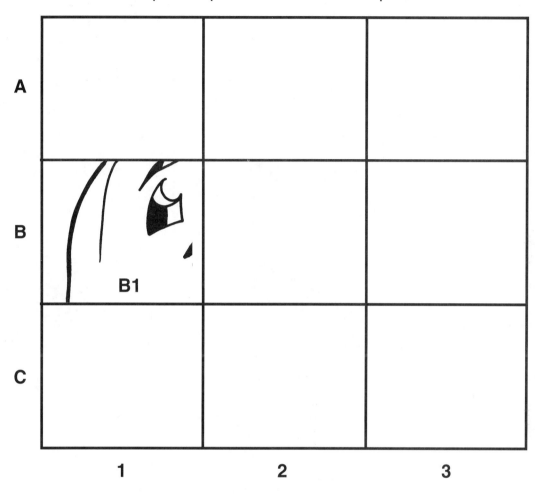

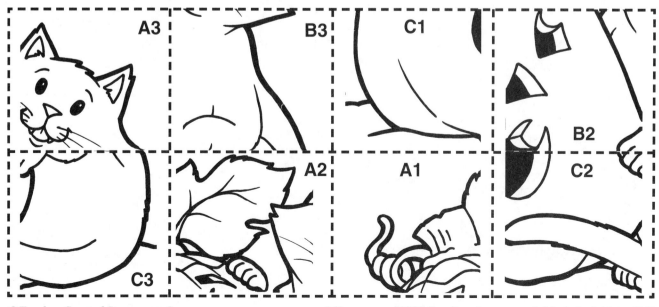

Pumpkin Sort

Directions: How many ways can the pumpkins be sorted?

Pumpkin Sort

To be in this family _____.

Costumes on Parade

Directions: Photocopy a class set of this page onto white construction paper. Then have students color and cut out the pictures and create different patterns. Glue each pattern onto a 12" length of sentence strip or a 3" x 12" piece of construction paper.

Costumes on Parade

Costumes on Parade

Name: _____

Bat Facts

Directions: Roll the dice. Write each number on the ears. Write the sum on the bat's forehead. Spin the spinner and compare the sum with the other player's sum. The winner for the round can color his or her bat.

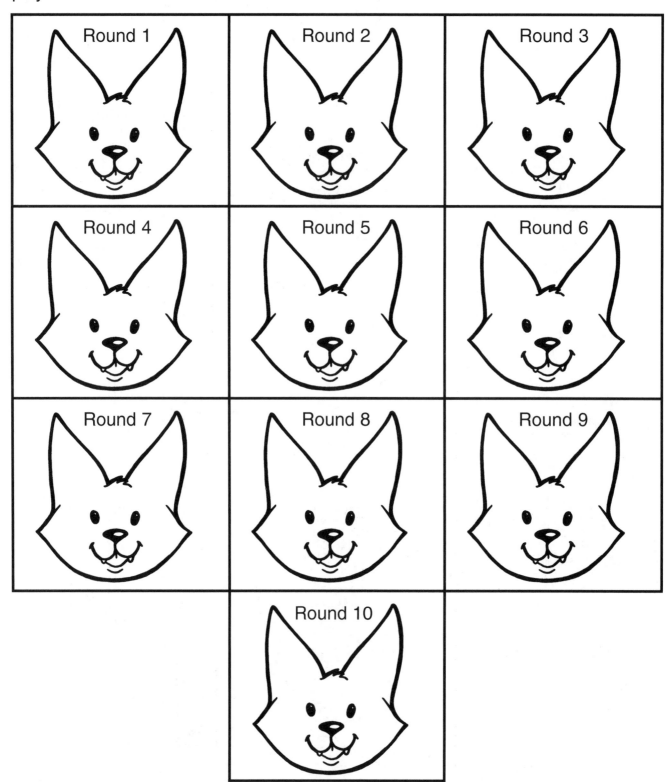

Bat Facts Spinners

Directions: Photocopy the spinners onto cardstock, laminate for durability, cut apart, and assemble the spinners.

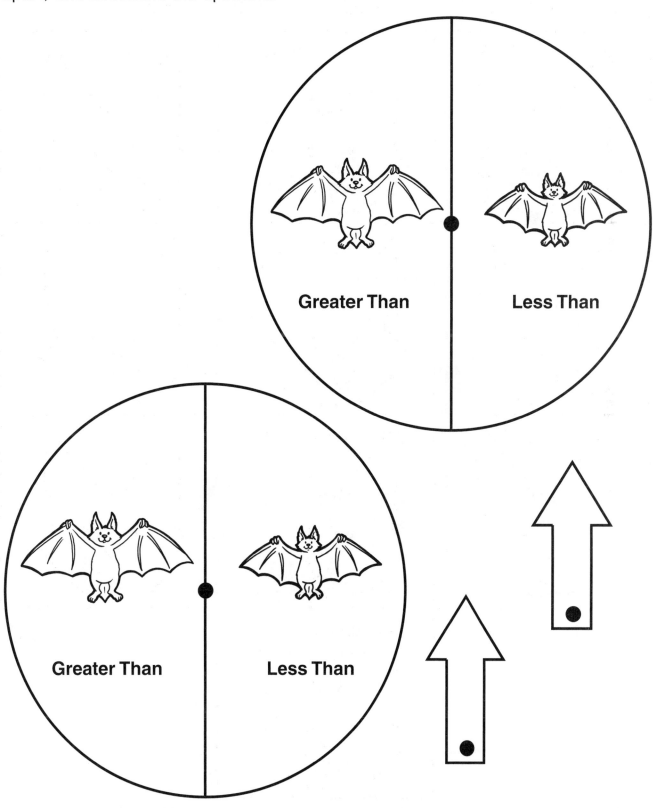

Bat Facts

Assembly Instructions for Number Die

1. Cut along all solid lines (including in and around large tabs).
2. Fold along all dashed lines.
3. Glue tab A to inside edge of side D.
4. Fold in top and bottom of flaps.

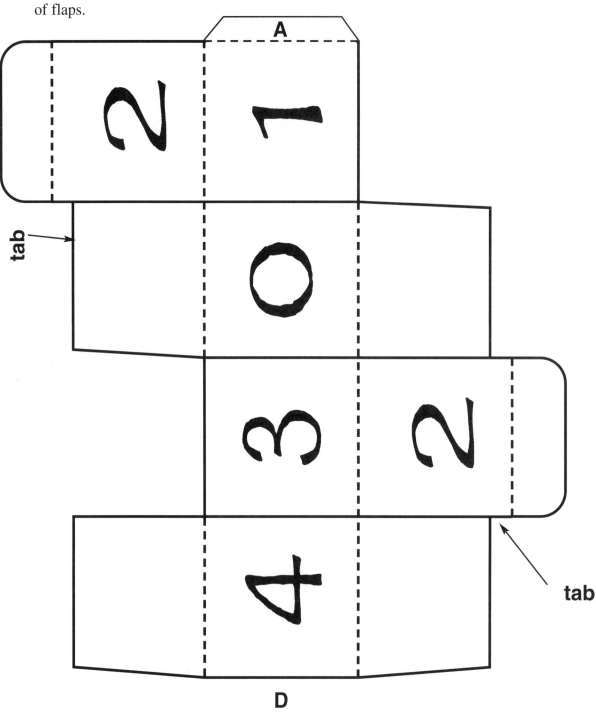

Bat Facts

Assembly Instructions for Picture Die

1. Cut along all solid lines (including in and around large tabs).
2. Fold along all dashed lines.
3. Glue tab A to inside edge of side D.
4. Fold in top and bottom flaps.

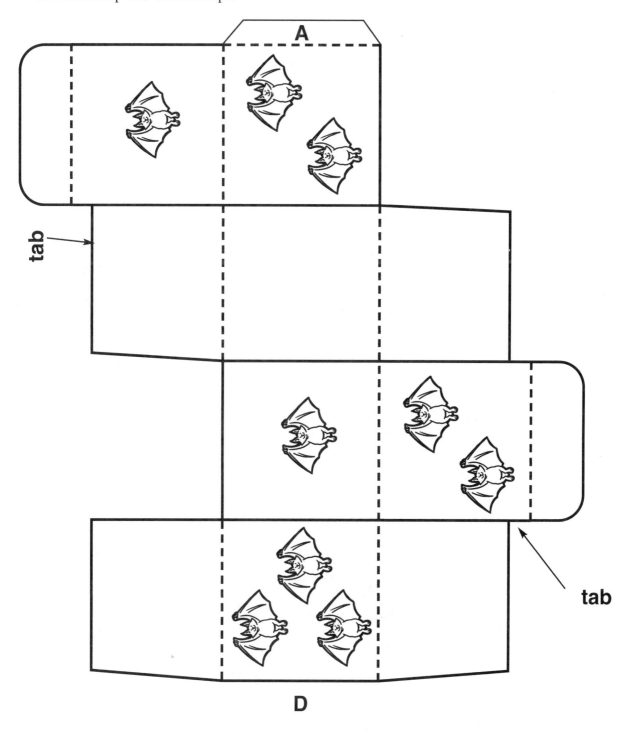

Number Match

Directions: Photocopy the numbers, number words, and picture cards onto cardstock or construction paper, color, laminate, and cut apart. For each student (or pair of students), provide one set of cards. Have the student lay the cards face up on the table in a 3 x 3 arrangement. Have the student look for two cards that match. After the student has picked up all of the cards that match, have the student fill in the 3 x 3 arrangement with the remaining cards in the stack. Continue in this manner until there are 11 cards left. Have the student place the 11 cards in order from 0 to 10. If playing with a partner, after the first student has found all of the matches, fill in the empty spaces with the unused cards and the second student may take his or her turn.

(*Teaching Tip:* The game can be made easier by using only two of the three number sets. For example, use only the number cards and the picture cards.)

zero

one two three

four

five

siX

seven

eight

nine

ten

Number Match

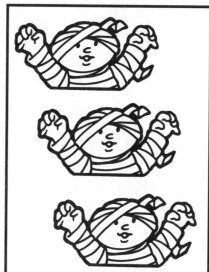

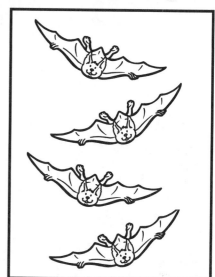

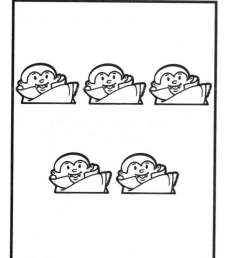

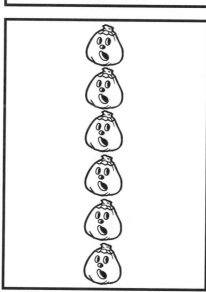

The Haunted House Game

5	3	2	0	4	

4 6					

4	2	3	5	3	1

					2

3	1	2	5	4	6

The Haunted House Game

2 4					

2	1	3	5	0	Start

Haunted House Game Markers and Cards

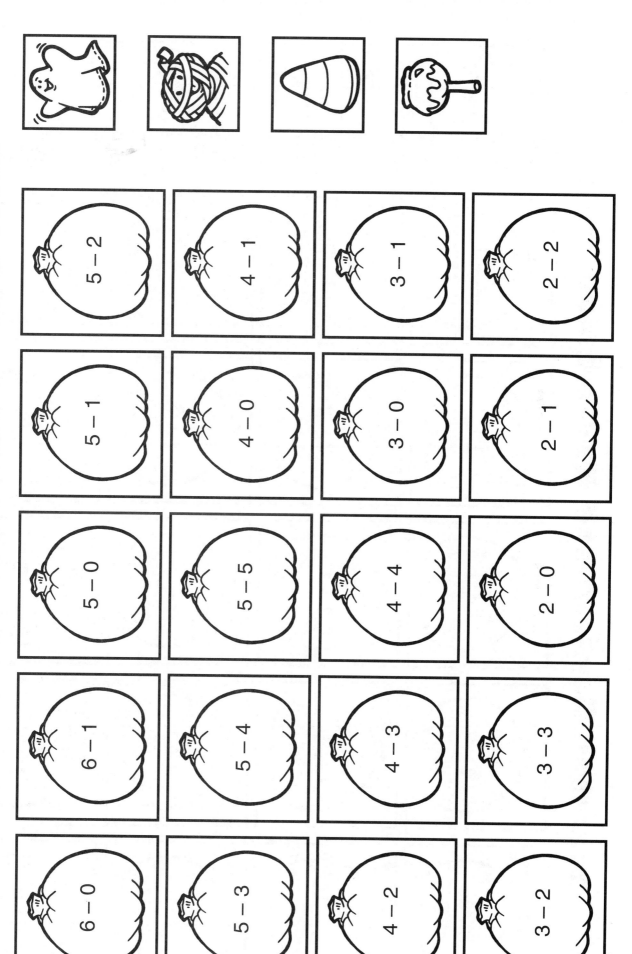

5 – 2 4 – 1 3 – 1 2 – 2

5 – 1 4 – 0 3 – 0 2 – 1

5 – 0 5 – 5 4 – 4 2 – 0

6 – 1 5 – 4 4 – 3 3 – 3

6 – 0 5 – 3 4 – 2 3 – 2

Haunted House Game Markers and Cards

4 + 1	3 + 3	2 + 4	1 + 4
4 + 0	3 + 2	2 + 3	1 + 3
5 + 1	3 + 1	2 + 2	1 + 2
5 + 0	3 + 0	2 + 1	1 + 1
6 + 0	4 + 2	2 + 0	1 + 0

Spider Man

Directions: Photocopy the spider, making enough copies for the class. Using the numbers 0–10, have each student write a number on the spider's stomach. Working with a partner, have each student roll the dice. If the total on the dice matches the number on the spider's stomach, the student records the math problem on one if the spider's legs and rolls again. If the total showing on the dice does not match the number on the spider's stomach, the student gives the dice to his or her partner. The first player to fill each leg with a math problem wins the game.

Variation #1: The student writes eight numbers in sequential order—one number for each leg. The student rolls the dice and must get the numbers in order before he or she can color that leg. The first player to color all of the spider's legs wins the game.

Variation #2: The student rolls the dice and records the math problem on one of the spider's legs. The first student to record eight math problems with eight different sums wins the game.

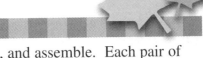

Spider Man

Directions: Photocopy the die pattern onto cardstock, color, laminate, and assemble. Each pair of students will need a pair of dice.

Assembly Instructions for Die

1. Cut along solid lines (including in and around large tabs).
2. Fold along all dashed lines.
3. Glue tab A to inside edge of side D.
4. Fold in top and bottom of flaps.

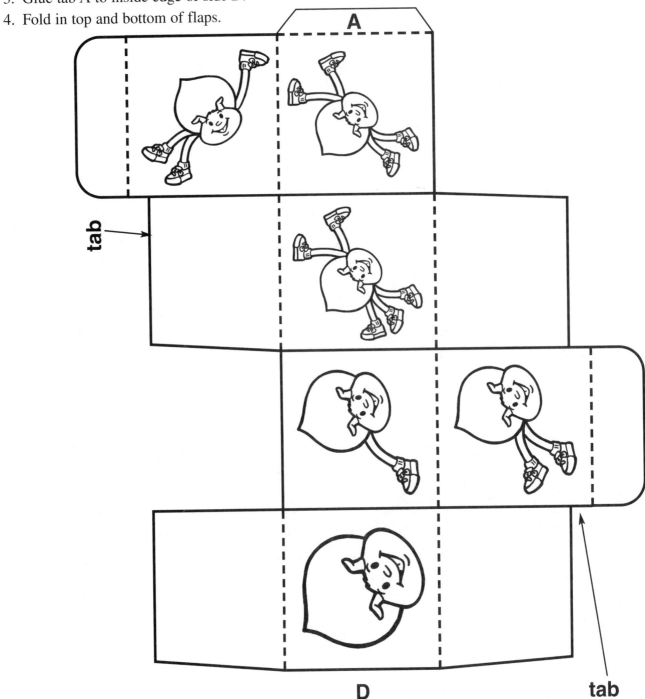

Answer Key

Page 134

Then: Took bread, meat, and water; Sailed on three small ships; Was a tough and scary voyage

Now: Enjoyed the journey and the scenery; Has a large kitchen with lots of different foods; Has one large ship with an engine

Statements will vary.

Page 135

Spiders: two body parts, eight legs, can go a year or more without eating

Insects: three body parts, six legs, has two antennas and might have wings

Statements will vary.

Page 136

Facts: Halloween is on October 31st; Some people go trick-or-treating; Pumpkins are a symbol of Halloween.

Opinions: Some costumes are scary; Halloween is fun; Halloween is the best holiday!

Statements will vary.

Page 137

1. candy
2. costume
3. jack-o-lantern
4. pumpkin
5. spider

Page 139

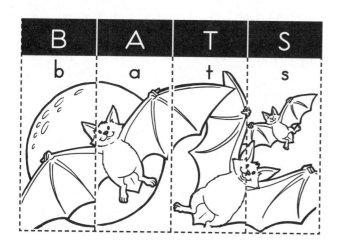

Page 140

Page 141

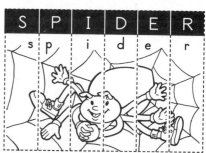

Page 142

Page 147

H	A	L	L	O	W	E	E	N	A	B	C	D	E
Q	P	R	S	W	W	I	T	C	H	E	S	P	F
G	O	T	U	L	A	B	M	O	O	N	N	O	G
H	B	A	T	S	Z	C	E	S	F	M	L	K	C
O	T	R	I	C	K	O	R	T	R	E	A	T	A
S	N	V	X	W	Y	D	P	U	M	P	K	I	N
T	M	H	O	U	S	E	S	M	G	H	I	J	D
S	P	I	D	E	R	S	L	E	K	J	I	H	Y

Page 148

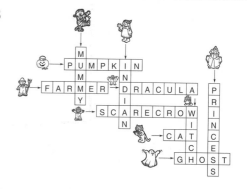

Answer Key

Page 149
1. candy corn
2. Dracula
3. jack-o-lantern
4. ghost
5. bat
6. web

Page 150
1. pumpkin
2. face
3. seeds
4. vine
5. stem
6. top

Page 154
black/white
over/under
pumpkin/jack-o-lantern
full/empty
happy/mad
asleep/awake

Page 155
1. over/under
2. awake/asleep
3. empty/full
4. black/white
5. jack-o-lantern/pumpkin
6. happy/mad

Page 156
1. October 12, 1492
2. 3
3. king and queen of Spain
4. spices

Page 157
1. dead relatives
2. skulls
3. altars

Page 158
1. fall
2. less carbon
3. live off its stored food
4. red

Page 159
1. fruits
2. giant pumpkin seeds
3. 365 pounds
4. melons

Page 160
1. bird of prey
2. turn its head
3. great gray owl
4. meat

Page 161
1. eight
2. fifteen years
3. two
4. arachnid

Page 162
1. bumblebee bat
2. just about anywhere
3. during the day

Page 163
1. pumpkin
2. scarecrow
3. cat

	Scarecrow	Cat	Pumpkin
Cleo	X	X	O
Stanley	O	X	X
Tom	X	O	X

Page 164
Frank
Answers will vary for clue.

Page 165
1. ghost = 4, cat = 1, pumpkin = 2, clown = 3
2. 2
3. 3
4. 1
5. 0
6. ghost

Page 166

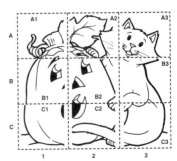

1. chocolate drops = 5, gum = 4, lollipops = 3
2. The picture of a chocolate drop should be circled.
3. The picture of gum should be circled.
4. The picture of a chocolate drop should be circled.
5. 12

Page 167
1. 8¢   2. 5¢   3. 1¢   4. 4¢   5. 3¢   6. 6¢

Page 169

November

Table of Contents

November

Introduction

November contains activities and games that cover monthly themes and events. The students will learn basic information about important November events. Through a variety of games and activities, the students will be able to practice important skills covered in the primary grades.

Language Activities

- **November Cover (page 192):** Simply photocopy the pages the students are to do and use this page as the cover for this unit. Or, photocopy sets of the writing paper for each student and staple to make a writing packet. The November cover can be used as the cover for the writing packet.
- **Activity Check-Off List (page 10):** This sheet can be used to keep track of each activity as it is completed by the student.
- **November Writing Prompts (pages 193 and 194):** Writing prompts for each one of the four domains are provided. The writing prompts are a fun way to explore November happenings!
- **Turkeys (page 195), On the Mayflower (page 196),** and **The First Thanksgiving (page 197):** These are cut-and-paste activities that have the students sort statements into different categories.
- **It's Time for Thanksgiving (page 198):** Students are sure to enjoy placing Thanksgiving vocabulary in the correct alphabetical order.
- **Native Americans and Food (page 199)** and **The Pilgrims' Voyage (page 200):** Students will learn about the life of the Native Americans and the Pilgrims. Pages can be cut apart and then stapled to make a mini-booklet.
- **Letter Matches (pages 201–203):** These cut-and-paste activities reinforce identifying and matching uppercase and lowercase letters. The students cut out the "puzzle pieces" at the bottom of the page and glue them in place under the matching uppercase letter. If done correctly, the letters will spell a word and a picture will be revealed.
- **Making Statements and Questions (page 204):** This activity contains rebus-like pictures and high-frequency words. The students cut apart the words and pictures and arrange and rearrange the words and pictures to make different questions and statements. When doing this activity with the whole class, an overhead transparency of the page can be made or use a photocopy machine to enlarge the words and pictures so that they can be easily seen by all of the students. Sample sentences that can be made are as follows:

    I see a turkey eating corn.   Where is the pilgrim?

- **How Many Words Can You Make? (page 205):** This activity is similar to "making words." The students cut apart the letter cards and arrange and rearrange the letters to make different words. When doing this activity with the whole class, make an overhead transparency of the page. Call on individual students to use the overhead to show the class a word he or she has made. This is also a great activity to send home with the students as homework. Sample words that can be made are as follows:

    Two-Letter Words: an, at, as, it   Four-Letter Words: tank, sank, sing
    Three-Letter Words: tan, sag, gas   Five- or More Letter Words: thanks, knight

- **Thanksgiving Word Search (page 206)** and **Native Americans (page 207):** Students will find vocabulary words about Thanksgiving in a word search or a crossword puzzle.
- **At Thanksgiving (page 208):** In this activity, students will learn more Thanksgiving vocabulary by placing labels underneath a picture.
- **Thanksgiving Bingo (pages 209–211):** Eight different bingo cards and matching calling cards are provided. Thanksgiving Bingo reinforces vocabulary and language development skills in a fun-filled, non-threatening manner.

November

Language Activities (cont.)

- **November Words (pages 212–214):** In this activity, students will use cards to put together words.
- **Veteran's Day (page 215), Turkeys (page 216),** and **The First Thanksgiving (page 217):** These pages provide basic background information on the topics for the student to read. There are several comprehension questions for each topic.

Math Activities

- **Plenty of Cornucopias (page 218):** Students will answer questions about a picture graph of cornucopias.
- **Time for Dinner! (page 219):** This activity helps students tell time on the hour.
- **Feathers (page 220):** Using an acorn ruler, students will measure the length of each feather.
- **Indian Teepee (page 221):** In this activity, students recognize and color shapes decorated on a teepee. Directions to assemble the teepee are also included.
- **What's for Dinner? (page 222):** For this activity, students use pattern blocks to make a turkey. The pattern has outlines showing the blocks that are to be used.
- **November Calendar (page 223 and 104):** Students will put together all the different parts of a calendar onto page 104 and then answer some questions about it.
- **Thanksgiving Puzzle (pages 224 and 225):** Cut out the puzzle squares on page 225. Find the answer to each puzzle square on page 224. Glue the puzzle square on top of the answer. If all of the problems have been answered correctly, a picture will be revealed.
- **Thanksgiving Patterns (page 226):** Each student will make patterns using different Thanksgiving pictures. For each student provide three to four 12" lengths of sentence strips and a photocopy of the pictures. Have the students use the pictures to create patterns on the sentence strips.
- **Turkeys in a Row (page 227):** In this activity, students use dice to create math problems. Students match the math problem to the answer on the turkey. The winner is the person who has a math problem for each turkey in the row!
- **Thanksgiving Playing Cards (pages 228–231):** In addition to the directions listed on page 228, the cards and spinners can be used to make addition problems and subtraction problems. To make addition and subtraction problems use the spinner on page 231. The player turns over two cards and then spins the spinner. The player records the matching math problem on a clean sheet of paper.
- **Subtracting Acorns (pages 232–234):** This activity can be played independently or in small groups. Taking turns, each student rolls the dice and records the subtraction sentence next to its answer. The first student to write a math problem for each number wins the game. (The dice for this activity are on pages 233 and 234.)
- **Turkey Hunt (pages 235–237):** Students will love to do math problems using this activity board game!
- **Add and Subtract (page 238):** This game is for a pair of students. Each pair of students will need one playing board (numbers 1–10), 20 counters (10 each of two different kinds or colors), and a spinner. Taking turns, each player spins the spinner and places the same number of counters on the playing board starting with the number 1. The players will be adding and taking counters from the board. The first player to use all of his or her counters wins the game. Examples of play: if there are four spaces left and a player rolls a 5, that player must take five counters off of the board and add them to his or her pile of counters. If there are five spaces left and player rolls a 5, but has only three counters, that player must take five counters off of the board. If there are five counters on the board, and the player rolls a 6, the player can not do anything! He or she cannot add six counters because there are not enough spaces left on the board and he or she cannot take off six counters because there are not enough counters on the board.

November Writing Prompts

Domain	Writing Prompt	Word Bank
Practical/Informative	How to Catch a Turkey	box, capture, chase, farm, forest, help, net, seed, trap
Practical/Informative	Parts of a Turkey	beak, crest, eye, feet, head, legs, wattle, wings
Practical/Informative	Nine Favorite Thanksgiving Foods	With the students, brainstorm a list of foods eaten at Thanksgiving.
Practical/Informative	Things to Do with the Leftover Turkey	With the students, brainstorm a list of ideas about what can be done with the leftovers.
Analytical/Expository	I am Thankful . . .	clothes, family, foods, friends, health, home, parents, warmth
Analytical/Expository	Would you liked to have sailed on the Mayflower?	adventure, dangerous, exciting, food, lonely, scary, seasick
Analytical/Expository	Do you like turkey?	delicious, meat, no, smells, tastes, wishbone, yes, yucky
Analytical/Expository	Should the turkey be the national bird?	With the students, brainstorm the pros and cons of having the turkey as the national bird.

November Writing Prompts

Domain	Writing Prompt	Word Bank
Imaginative/Narrative	Save Me! (a turkey)	animal, eat, escape, forest, help, net, run, set free, trap
Imaginative/Narrative	What would it be like to live in a teepee?	adventure, camp, cozy, design, easy to move, fun, noisy, sticks, tree house, village
Imaginative/Narrative	My Life as a Pilgrim	field, friends, gather, hard, harvest, Indians, sailing, ships, travel, water, work
Imaginative/Narrative	You can only communicate through smoke signals. What would you say?	air, clouds, emergency, fire, hunting, need help, read, seen, signals, smoke
Sensory/Descriptive	What is your favorite thing about Thanksgiving?	cooking, cousins, family, food, football, friends, games, kitchen, relatives, smells
Sensory/Descriptive	How do you feel after eating a big Thanksgiving meal?	full, great, happy, sick, sleepy, stuffed, tired, unbutton pants
Sensory/Descriptive	Describe the perfect turkey. (real or cooked!)	big, delicious, feathers, golden, juicy, meaty, plump, round, runs, small, tender
Sensory/Descriptive	Wishbone Wishes	With the students, brainstorm a list of things for which the students might wish.

Turkeys

Directions: Cut out the statements in the boxes at the bottom of the page. Glue them under the correct title.

Facts	Opinions

Directions: Write another true statement about turkeys.

_____

- -

_____

_____

- -

_____

Turkeys make great pets.	Turkeys are birds.
Turkeys have feathers.	Turkeys are delicious to eat.
Turkeys are fun to play with.	Turkeys can be wild or domesticated.

On the Mayflower

Directions: Cut out the words in the boxes at the bottom of the page. Glue them under the correct title.

Items Taken on the Mayflower	Items Not Taken on the Mayflower

Directions: Write another true statement about an item taken on the Mayflower.

_____

- -

_____

_____

- -

_____

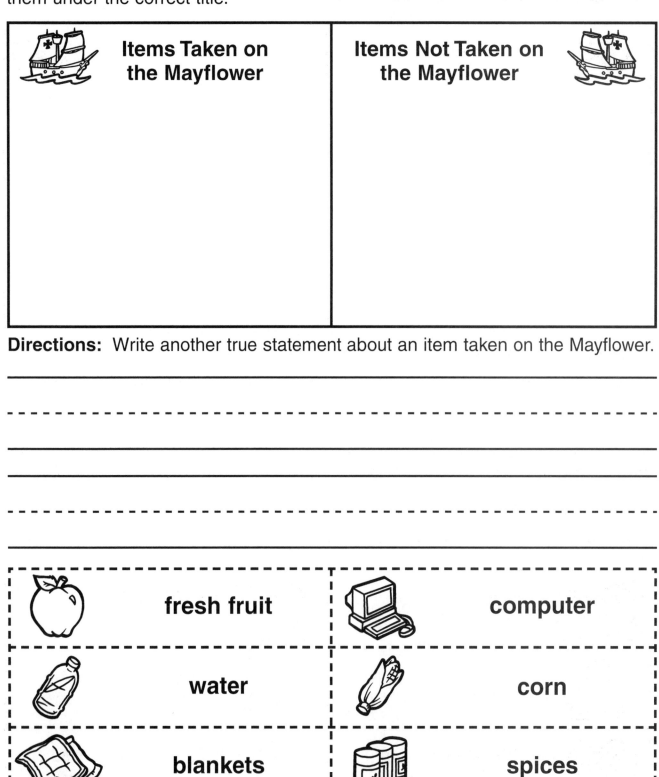

fresh fruit	computer
water	corn
blankets	spices

The First Thanksgiving

Directions: Cut out the statements in the boxes at the bottom of the page. Glue them under the correct title.

True	False

Directions: Write another true statement about the first Thanksgiving.

_____

- - - - - - - - - - - - - - - - - -

_____

_____

- - - - - - - - - - - - - - - - - -

_____

	Pilgrims and Indians celebrated together.		The Indians and Pilgrims were friends.
	The Indians did not come to the feast.		The Indians brought popcorn to the feast.
	The Pilgrims made French fries.		The Pilgrims had a bountiful harvest.

It's Time for Thanksgiving

Directions: Cut out and glue the picture and word cards in alphabetical order.

1.

2.

3.

4.

5.

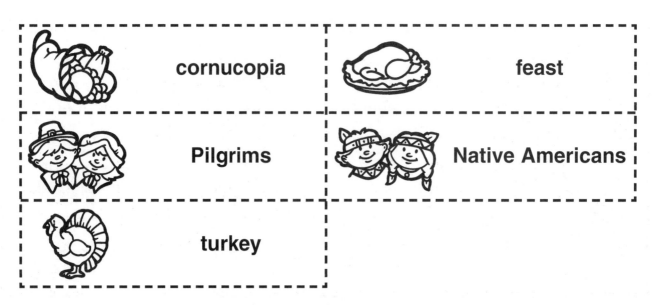

cornucopia

feast

Pilgrims

Native Americans

turkey

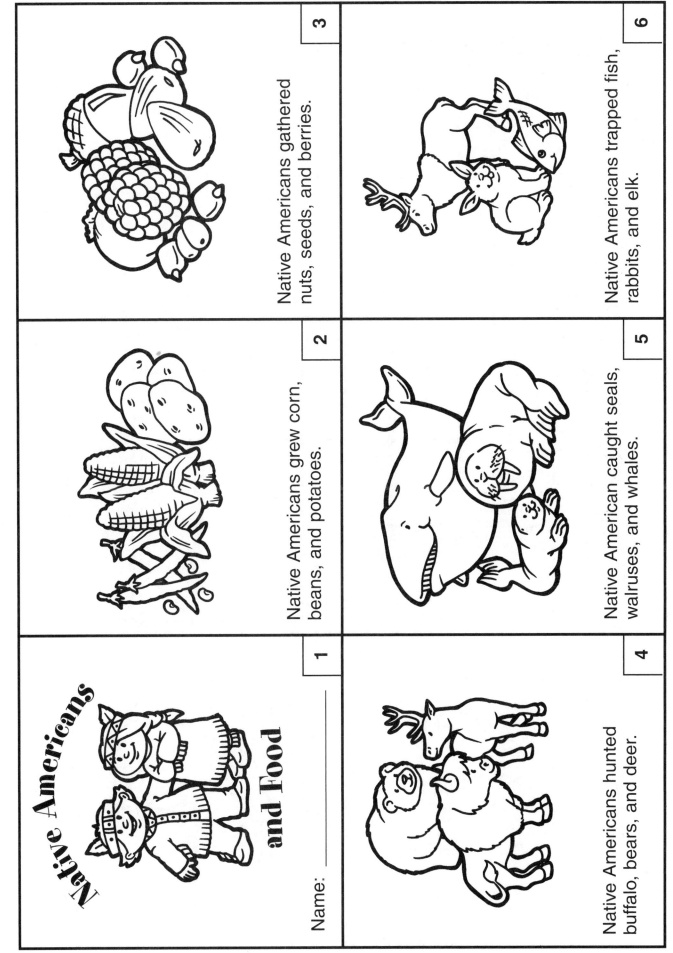

3 Native Americans gathered nuts, seeds, and berries.

6 Native Americans trapped fish, rabbits, and elk.

2 Native Americans grew corn, beans, and potatoes.

5 Native American caught seals, walruses, and whales.

Native Americans and Food

1 Name: _____

4 Native Americans hunted buffalo, bears, and deer.

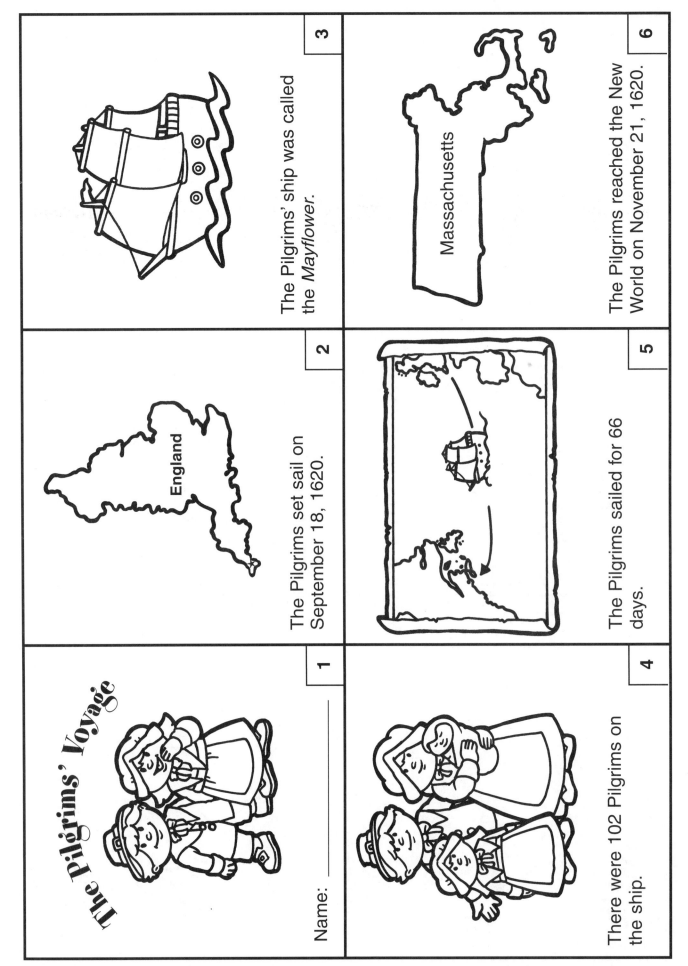

3

The Pilgrims' ship was called the *Mayflower*.

6

Massachusetts

The Pilgrims reached the New World on November 21, 1620.

2

England

The Pilgrims set sail on September 18, 1620.

5

The Pilgrims sailed for 66 days.

1

The Pilgrims' Voyage

Name: _____

4

There were 102 Pilgrims on the ship.

Letter Match

Directions: Cut out the boxes at the bottom of the page. Glue the lowercase letter box to the uppercase letter box to find a picture.

A	C	O	R	N

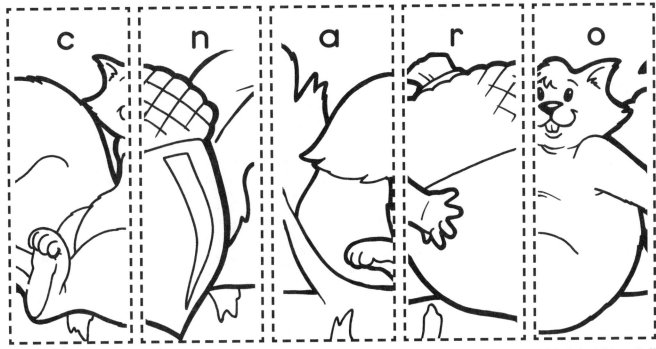

Letter Match

Directions: Cut out the boxes at the bottom of the page. Glue the lowercase letter box to the uppercase letter box to find a picture.

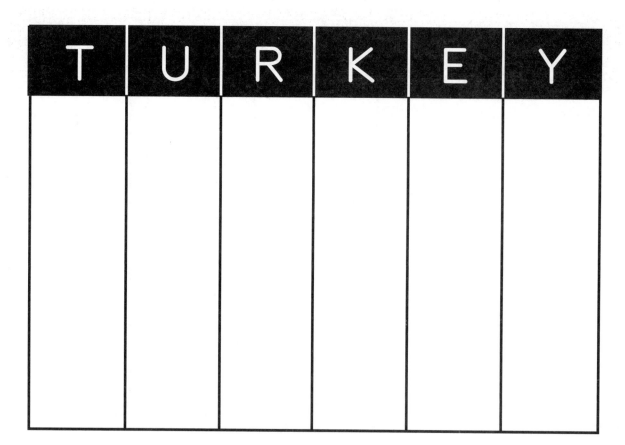

T	U	R	K	E	Y

| e | k | r | t | u | y |

Letter Match

Directions: Cut out the boxes at the bottom of the page. Glue the lowercase letter box to the uppercase letter box to find a picture.

M	A	Y	F	L	O	W	E	R

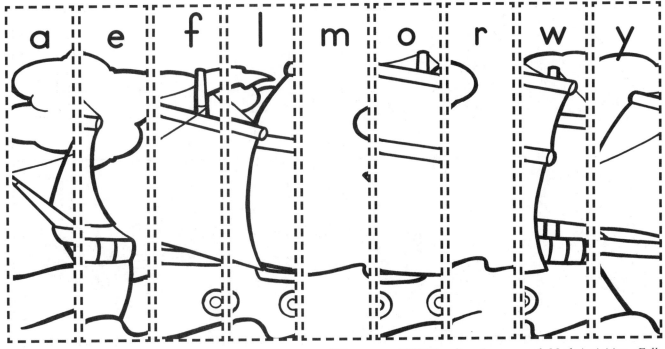

a	e	f	l	m	o	r	w	y

 #3888 Reading, Language & Math Activities: Fall

Making Statements and Questions

Directions: Cut out the cards and create statements and questions.

is	Where	.	¿
pilgrim	round	the	does
feathers	Native American	a	have
pumpkin	turkey	I	has
see	eating	corn	

How Many Words Can You Make?

Directions: Cut out the letters at the bottom of the page. Rearrange the letters to make different words. Write each word under the correct heading.

2-Letter Words	3-Letter Words	4-Letter Words	5-or-More-Letter Words

T	H	A	N	K	S	G	I	V	I	N	G

©Teacher Created Resources, Inc.   205   #3888 Reading, Language & Math Activities: Fall

Thanksgiving Word Search

Directions: Find and color each word. Color the remaining Xs, Ys, and Zs to find a secret message from Tom the Turkey.

CORN
FRIENDS
HARVEST
INDIANS
MAYFLOWER

PILGRIMS
PLYMOUTH
TEEPEE
THANKSGIVING
TURKEY

P	I	L	G	R	I	M	S	X	Y	Z	X
X	Y	Z	X	P	L	Y	M	O	U	T	H
Z	F	R	I	E	N	D	S	Y	Z	X	Y
T	H	A	N	K	S	G	I	V	I	N	G
G	O	B	B	L	E	C	O	R	N	Y	Z
Y	Z	I	N	D	I	A	N	S	X	Z	X
H	A	R	V	E	S	T	X	Z	Y	X	Y
G	O	B	B	L	E	T	U	R	K	E	Y
X	Y	X	T	E	E	P	E	E	Z	Y	Z
M	A	Y	F	L	O	W	E	R	Z	Y	X

Native Americans

Directions: Complete the crossword puzzle.

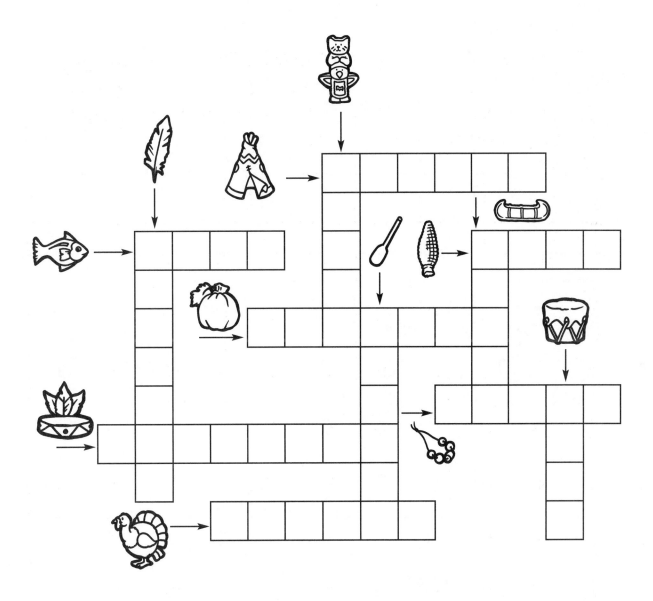

BEADS   FEATHER   PUMPKIN

CANOE   FISH   TEEPEE

CORN   HEADBAND   TOTEM

DRUM   PADDLE   TURKEY

At Thanksgiving

Directions: Glue each word under the correct picture.

1.

2.

3.

4.

5.

6.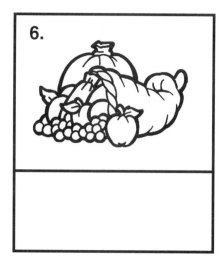

cornucopia	Pilgrim
turkey dinner	scarecrow
Native American	turkey

Bingo Cards

Card 1

Thanksgiving Bingo

headband	Indians	drum
cornucopia	Free Space	leaf
Pilgrims	Mayflower	turkey

Card 2

Thanksgiving Bingo

Indians	turkey	Mayflower
hat	Free Space	headband
acorn	Pilgrims	leaf

Card 3

Thanksgiving Bingo

hat	Indians	headband
pumpkin	Free Space	acorn
drum	feather	cornucopia

Card 4

Thanksgiving Bingo

acorn	drum	turkey
hat	Free Space	Pilgrims
Mayflower	leaf	Indians

Bingo Cards

Thanksgiving Bingo

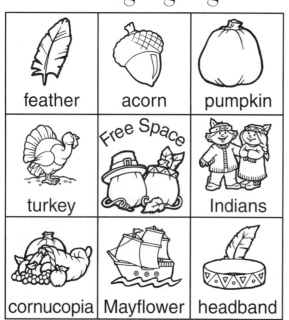

feather	acorn	pumpkin
turkey	Free Space	Indians
cornucopia	Mayflower	headband

Thanksgiving Bingo

Indians	hat	pumpkin
feather	Free Space	drum
acorn	Pilgrims	cornucopia

Thanksgiving Bingo

headband	acorn	feather
leaf	Free Space	pumpkin
Mayflower	turkey	hat

Thanksgiving Bingo

leaf	Pilgrims	cornucopia
feather	Free Space	hat
turkey	pumpkin	drum

Bingo Calling Cards

feather	headband	hat
turkey	Pilgrims	drum
leaf	pumpkin	acorn
Mayflower	cornucopia	Indians

November Words

Photocopy the pictures onto cardstock or construction paper, color, laminate, and cut apart. To play the game, follow the directions below:

1. Shuffle the cards and place in a stack face down with one card turned face up on the table.
2. Working with a partner, have one student turn over the top card.
3. If the card can be combined with any other card(s) already face up on the table, the student may take the two cards that make a complete word and take another turn. If no word can be made, the student leaves his or her card face up on the table.
4. The next student takes his or her turn.
5. The student with the most matches wins the game.

Variation (Play Concentration!): Shuffle all of the cards and arrange them face down in a 5 x 4 array. Taking turns, each student turns over two cards. If the cards make a word, the student may keep both cards and takes another turn. If the cards do not match, the student returns them to their original places and play continues with the next player. The student with the most matches wins the game.

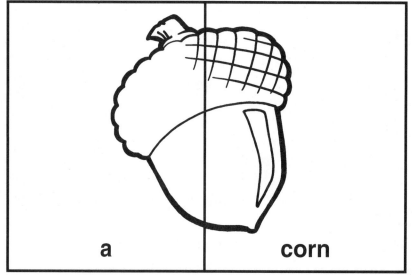

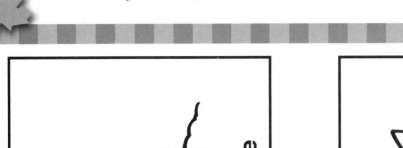

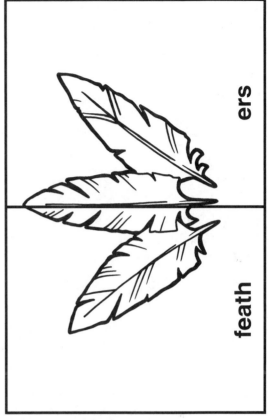

pee

tee

ers

feath

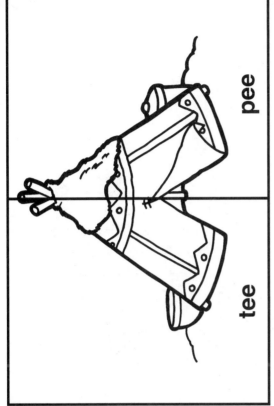

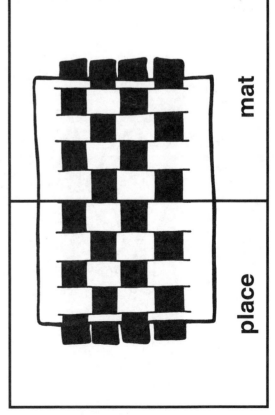

grims

Pil

mat

place

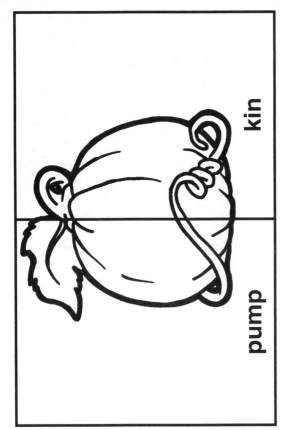

pump · kin

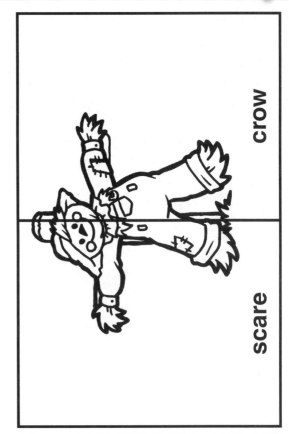

scare · crow

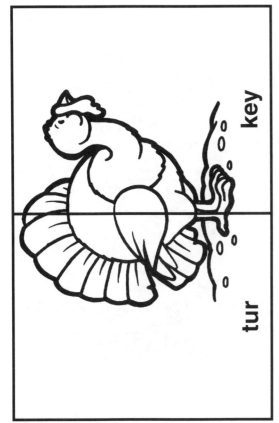

tur · key

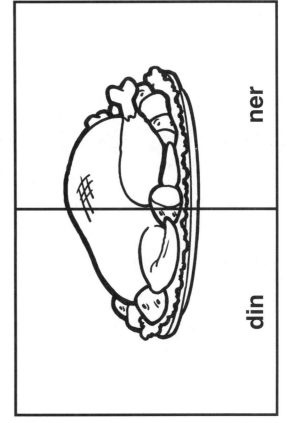

din · ner

Veteran's Day

On November 11th, the United States, France, and England buried an unknown soldier in each nation's highest place of honor. The three countries did this to honor and recognize all of the people who had fought in World War I. This day was known as Armistice Day.

In 1954, President Eisenhower signed a bill proclaiming November 11th as Veteran's Day. President Eisenhower did this to recognize all of the Americans who had served in all wars, not just World War I.

Directions: Answer the questions. Fill in the correct answer circle.

1. What day is Veteran's Day?

November 11   1954   World War I

◯   ◯   ◯

2. When did President Eisenhower sign the proclamation?

1953   1955   1954

◯   ◯   ◯

3. Who is buried in each nation's highest place of honor?

a flag   an unknown soldier   a medal

◯   ◯   ◯

4. Whom does Veteran's Day recognize?

all war veterans   World War II veterans   Desert Storm veterans

◯   ◯   ◯

Turkeys

Turkeys can be wild or domesticated. People take care of domesticated turkeys. Turkeys eat berries, nuts, insects, and small lizards.

Turkeys have a fleshy growth that hangs down from their throats. It is called a **wattle**. Turkeys also have a **snood**. A snood is a fleshy growth that drapes over their beaks.

Male turkeys are called **toms** or **gobblers**. Female turkeys are called hens. Baby turkeys are called **poults.**

Directions: Answer the questions. Fill in the correct answer circle.

1. What do turkeys eat?

berries ○   leaves ○   bark ○

2. What are baby turkeys called?

chicks ○   poults ○   roosters ○

3. What is the fleshy growth that hangs over a turkey's beak?

a wattle ○   a crest ○   a snood ○

4. What is one kind of turkey?

domesticated ○   tame ○   free ○

The First Thanksgiving

Just about every culture in the world has a celebration giving thanks for having a bountiful harvest. In the fall of 1621, the Pilgrims invited the local Indian chief and 90 Indians to help give thanks for having bountiful crops of corn, barley, beans, and pumpkins.

The Indians brought deer, turkeys, cranberries, corn, and squash. The Indians showed Pilgrims different ways of cooking the fruits and vegetables. There was not any popcorn at the first Thanksgiving.

Directions: Answer the questions. Fill in the correct answer circle.

1. What was not served at the first Thanksgiving?

corn   ◯

cranberries   ◯

popcorn   ◯

2. When was the first Thanksgiving held?

1621   ◯

1690   ◯

1261   ◯

3. For what were the Pilgrims thankful?

a bountiful harvest   ◯

a good hunting trip   ◯

being in America   ◯

4. What did the Pilgrims learn to prepare from the Indians?

fruits and vegetables   ◯

cakes and puddings   ◯

popcorn and salad   ◯

Plenty of Cornucopias

	MON.	TUES.	WED.	THURS.	FRI.
6		🌽			
5		🌽		🌽	
4		🌽		🌽	
3	🌽	🌽		🌽	🌽
2	🌽	🌽	🌽	🌽	🌽
1	🌽	🌽	🌽	🌽	🌽

Directions: Use the graph to answer each question.

1. How many cornucopias were sold on Wednesday? _____

2. Were there more cornucopias sold on Monday or on Tuesday? _____

3. Which day were the fewest cornucopias sold? _____

4. Which day were the most cornucopias sold? _____

Directions: Solve each math problem.

5. Thursday – Friday = _____

6. Wednesday + Monday = _____

7. Tuesday – Friday = _____

8. Wednesday + Thursday = _____s

Time for Dinner!

Directions: Write the time on the line.

1.	2.	3.
___ : ___ ___	___ : ___ ___	___ : ___ ___
4.	5.	6.
___ : ___ ___	___ : ___ ___	___ : ___ ___
7.	8.	9.
___ : ___ ___	___ : ___ ___	___ : ___ ___

Feathers

Directions: Cut out the acorn ruler. Use the ruler to measure the length of each feather.

1. The feather is _____ acorns long.   **2.** The feather is _____ acorns long.

3. The feather is _____ acorns long.   **4.** The feather is _____ acorns long.

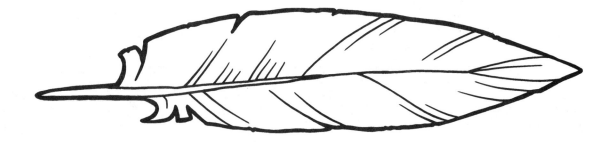

5. The feather is _____ acorns long

Indian Teepee

Directions: Color the teepee.

◇ = blue

△ = red

☆ = yellow

▯ = green

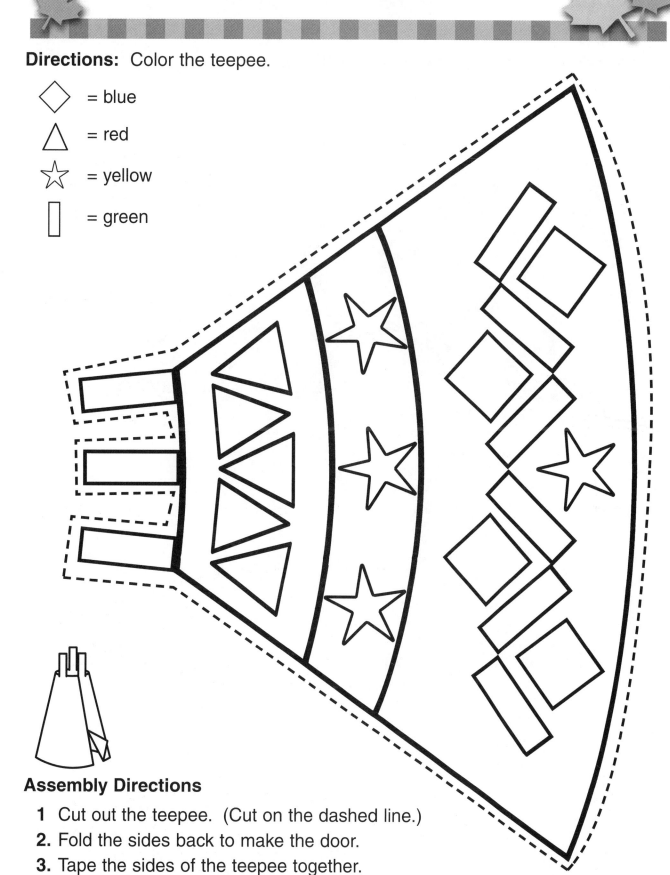

Assembly Directions

1. Cut out the teepee. (Cut on the dashed line.)
2. Fold the sides back to make the door.
3. Tape the sides of the teepee together.

What's for Dinner?

Directions: Fill in the shape with pattern blocks.

_____ for dinner!

I used the following number of shapes:

1. _____

2. _____

3. _____

4. _____

5. _____

6. _____

November Calendar

Directions: Photocopy the blank calendar (page 104) and the calendar "fill-ins" on this page. (Note: Make a clean copy of the calendar fill-in page first and add any special school or local events. The students' names can be added to the birthday squares. Then photocopy the completed "fill-in" page.) Have the students add the month and the days of the week to the calendar. The students can also write the current year next to the name of the month. Have the students write the calendar numbers in each square. Have the students add the special squares to the appropriate dates on the calendar. Using markers or crayons, have the students color the calendar. Then have the students answer the questions about the calendars.

(*Optional Step:* Fold a 12" x 18" inch piece of colored construction paper in half which is 12" x 9". Have the students open the folded piece of construction paper and glue or staple the completed calendar to the bottom half of the paper. On the top half, have the students draw a picture for the current month.)

Calendar "Fill-ins"

Veteran's Day	Thanksgiving				Thursday	Wednesday
11						Sunday
						Saturday
birthday	birthday	birthday				Tuesday
						Friday
						Monday

NOVEMBER

Calendar Questions

1. What is the name of the month? _____

2. What is the year? _____

3. How many days are in the month? _____

4. On what day does the month begin? _____

5. On what day does the month end? _____

6. How many days are in one week? _____

7. How many Wednesdays are in the month? _____

8. How many birthdays are there? _____

9. What is the date for Thanksgiving? _____

Thanksgiving Puzzle

Directions: Cut out the squares on page 225 and glue them to the matching answer below. If the answers are placed correctly, a picture will appear.

6	0	4
2	**8**	**5**
3	**1**	**7**

Thanksgiving Puzzle

Directions: Cut out the squares below and glue them to the matching answer on page 224. If the answers are placed correctly, a picture will appear.

8 − 1   6 − 2   6 − 5

4 − 4   7 − 4   7 − 1

8 − 3   8 − 0   5 − 3

Thanksgiving Patterns

Directions: Photocopy a class set of this page onto white construction paper. Have the students color, cut out the pictures, and arrange the pictures into different patterns. Glue the pictures onto a 12" piece of sentence strip.

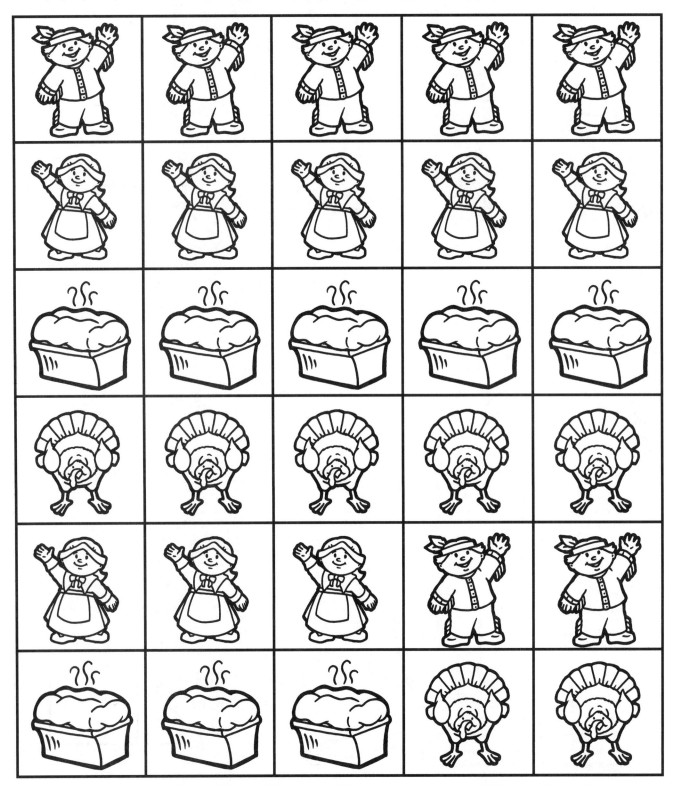

Turkeys in a Row

Directions: Photocopy one playing board for each student.

To Play The Game

1. Taking turns, have each student roll two six-sided dice. Have the student count the number of dots showing on the dice and write the math problem under the matching answer. (Example: The student rolls a 4 and a 3. Under the turkey with the number 7, the student writes 3 + 4.)

2. To win the game, the student must have a math problem for each one of the turkeys.

Variations

- Use double-six dominoes instead of dice. The student selects a domino, counts the number of pips, and records the math problem under the turkey with the answer.

- Provide each group of students with two sets of 3" x 5" flash cards with the following numbers: 1, 2, 3, 4, 5, 6. Taking turns, each student takes the top two cards from the stack and records the math problem under the correct turkey.

Turkeys in a Row

2	3	4	5	6	7	8	9	10	11	12

Thanksgiving Playing Cards

Directions: Photocopy two sets (or more) of the playing cards and the desired spinner for each pair of students. Have the students divide the cards. Both students turn over the top card of his or her deck. One student spins the spinner. The student who has the card corresponding to the spinner wins the round and keeps both cards. When a student runs out of cards, he or she can shuffle the cards he or she has won and start with a fresh deck. The winner is the student who ends up with all of the playing cards.

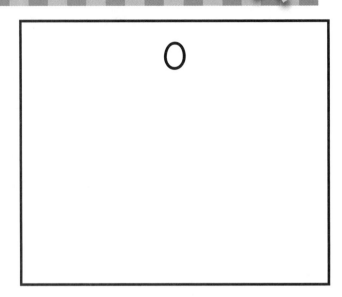

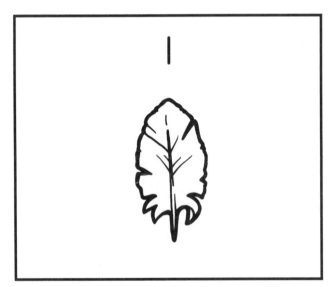

Thanksgiving Playing Cards

5

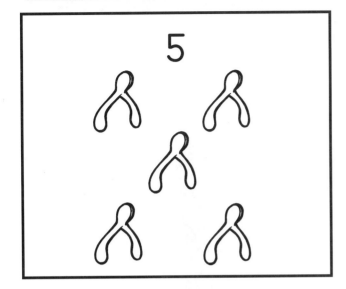

6

7

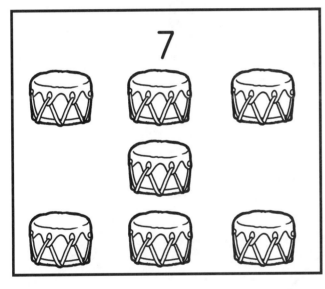

8

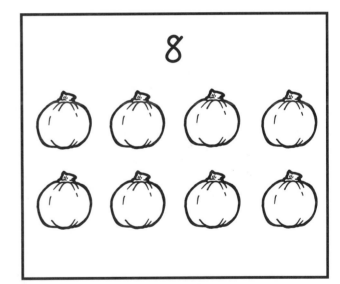

9

10

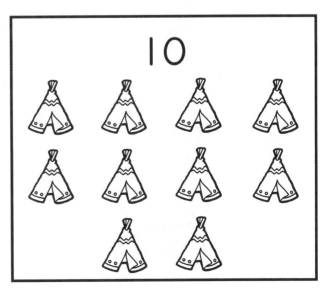

229 #3888 Reading, Language & Math Activities: Fall

Thanksgiving Playing Cards

Spinners

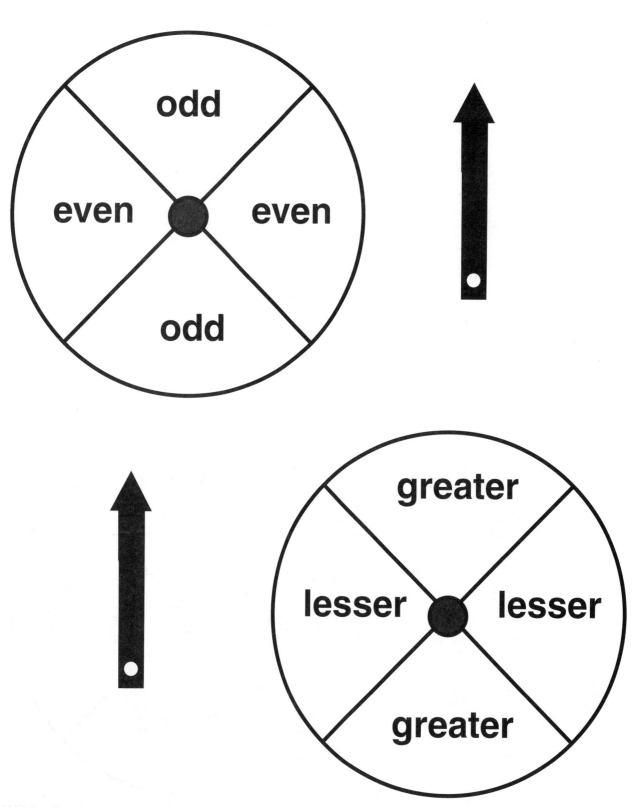

Thanksgiving Playing Cards

Spinners

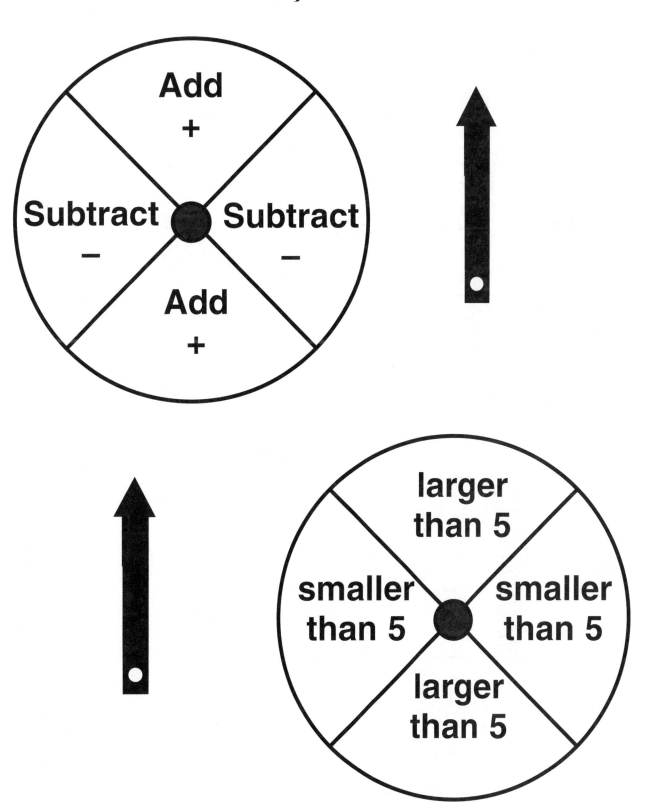

Subtracting Acorns

Directions: Take turns rolling the dice. Create a subtraction sentence with the dice. Record the subtraction sentence next to its answer. The first student to write a math problem for each number wins the game.

0	
1	
2	
3	
4	
5	
6	
7	
8	
9	
10	

Subtracting Acorns
(Picture Dice)

Assembly Instructions

1. Cut along all solid lines (including in and around large tabs.)
2. Fold along all dashed lines.
3. Glue tab A to inside edge of Side D.
4. Fold in top and bottom flaps.

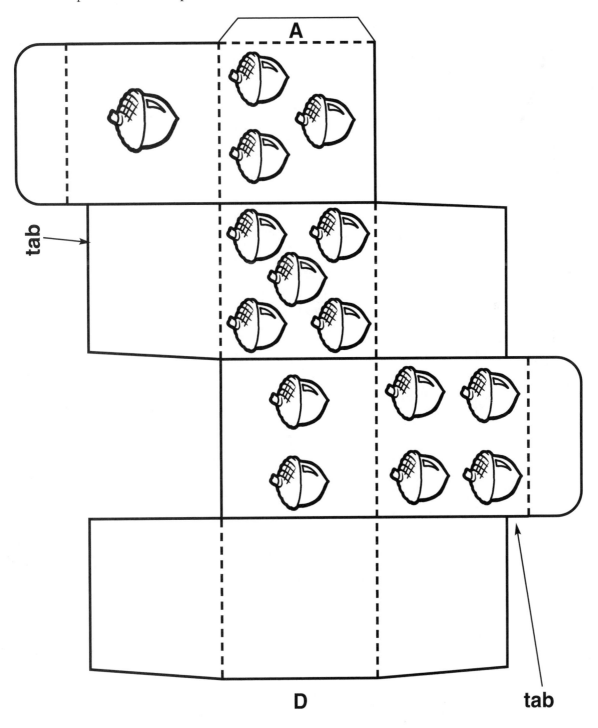

Subtracting Acorns
(Number Dice)

Assembly Instructions

1. Cut along all solid lines (including in and around large tabs.)
2. Fold along all dashed lines.
3. Glue tab A to inside edge of Side D.
4. Fold in top and bottom flaps.

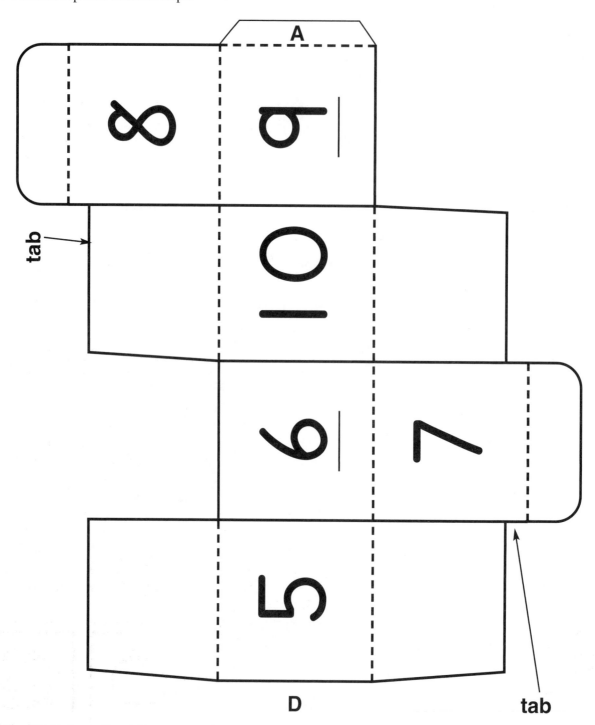

Turkey Hunt

Directions: Photocopy the playing board, game pieces, and math problems onto cardstock or construction paper. Color, laminate, and cut apart.

To Play the Game: Shuffle the math problems and place in a stack face down. The first player takes a card, solves the math problem, and moves to the nearest space with the matching answer. If a player should land in the same space as another player, the player who was there first, gets bumped back to start. The winner is the first player to land on the space right next to the turkey.

Shortcuts: If a player lands on a space with a ladder, the player can climb down (or up) the ladder to the other space.

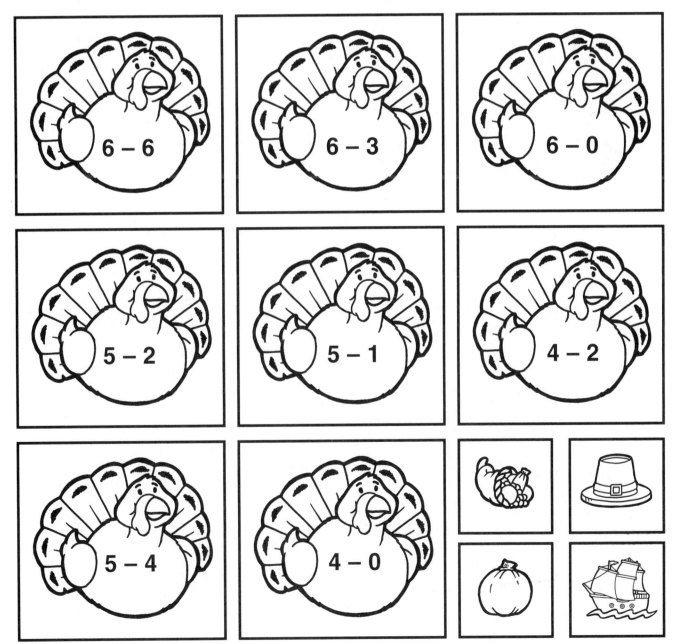

Turkey Hunt

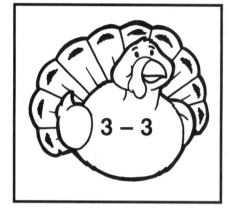
3 – 3

3 – 1

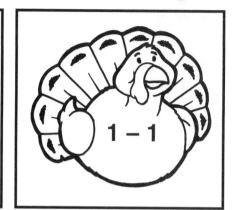
1 – 1

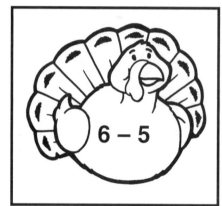
6 – 5

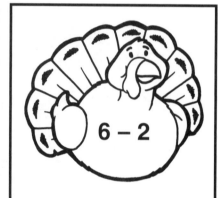
6 – 2

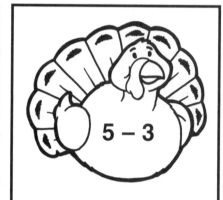
5 – 3

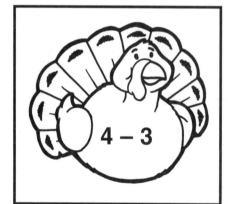
4 – 3

2 – 2

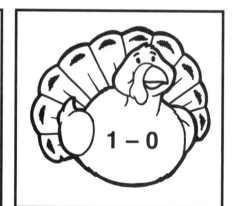
1 – 0

0 – 0

0 – 0

5 – 0

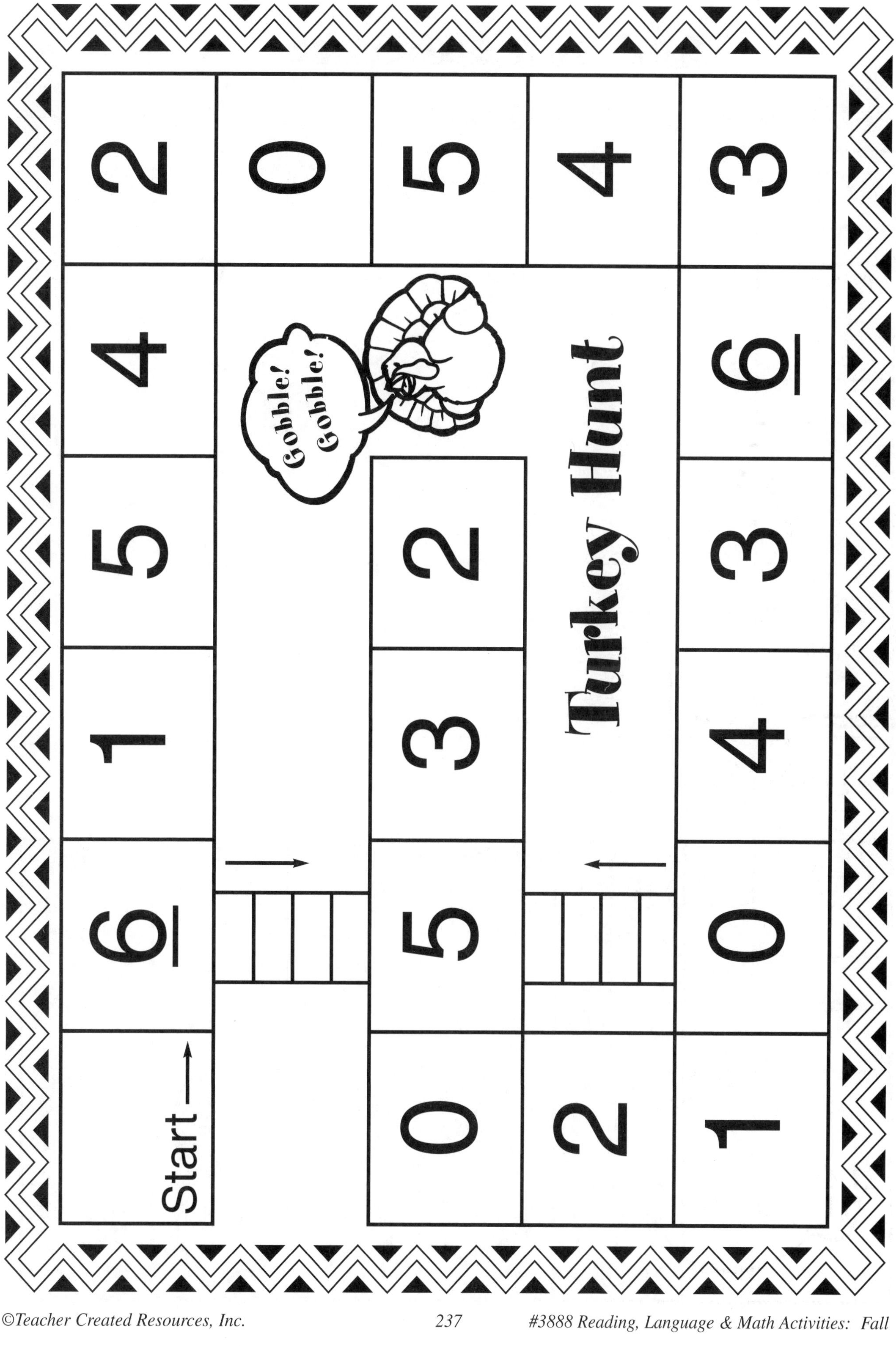

Start →

2 0 5 4 3

4 5 1 6

Gobble! Gobble!

2 3 5 6

Turkey Hunt

4 3 6

0 1 2 0

Add and Subtract

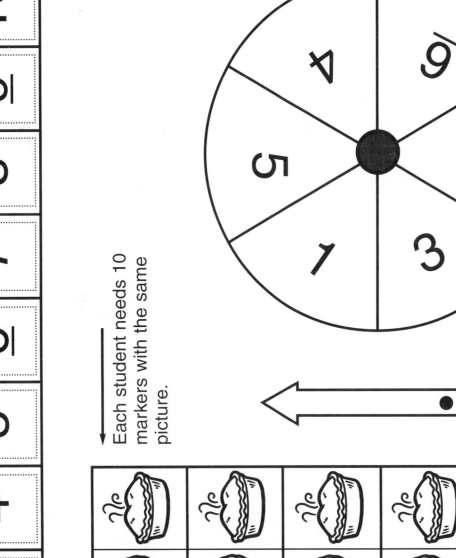

Each student needs 10 markers with the same picture.

Answer Key

Page 195

Facts

Turkeys have feathers.

Turkeys are birds.

Turkeys can be wild or domesticated.

Opinions

Turkeys make great pets.

Turkeys are fun to play with.

Turkeys are delicious to eat.

Statements will vary.

Page 196

Items Taken on the Mayflower: water, spices, blankets

Items Not Taken on the Mayflower: computer, corn, fresh fruit

Page 197

True

The Indians and Pilgrims were friends.

The Pilgrims had a bountiful harvest.

Pilgrims and Indians celebrated together.

False

The Pilgrims made French fries.

The Indians brought popcorn to the feast.

The Indians did not come to the feast.

Statements will vary.

Page 198

1. cornucopia
2. feast
3. Native Americans
4. Pilgrims
5. turkey

Page 201

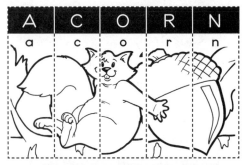

Page 202

Page 203

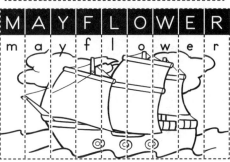

Page 206

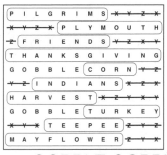

Secret message: GOBBLE GOBBLE

Page 207

Answer Key

Page 208
1. Pilgrim
2. Native American
3. scarecrow
4. turkey dinner
5. turkey
6. cornucopia

Page 215
1. November 11
2. 1954
3. an unknown soldier
4. all war veterans

Page 216
1. berries
2. poults
3. a snood
4. domesticated

Page 217
1. popcorn
2. 1621
3. a bountiful harvest
4. fruits and vegetables

Page 218
1. 2
2. Tuesday
3. Wednesday
4. Tuesday
5. $5 - 3 = 2$
6. $2 + 3 = 5$
7. $6 - 3 = 3$
8. $2 + 5 = 7$

Page 219
1. 3:00
2. 11:00
3. 6:00
4. 10:00
5. 1:00
6. 4:00
7. 9:00
8. 2:00
9. 7:00

Page 220
1. 3
2. 3
3. 4
4. 1
5. 6

Page 222
1. 3
2. 0
3. 0
4. 10
5. 1
6. 1

Page 224